FAMOUS AUTHORS FOR YOUNG PEOPLE

Famous Biographies for Young People

FAMOUS VIOLINISTS FOR YOUNG PEOPLE

FAMOUS PIANISTS FOR YOUNG PEOPLE

FAMOUS COMPOSERS FOR YOUNG PEOPLE

MODERN COMPOSERS FOR YOUNG PEOPLE

FAMOUS AUTHORS FOR YOUNG PEOPLE

FAMOUS PIONEERS FOR YOUNG PEOPLE

FAMOUS EXPLORERS FOR YOUNG PEOPLE

FAMOUS GENERALS AND ADMIRALS FOR YOUNG PEOPLE

FAMOUS KINGS AND QUEENS FOR YOUNG PEOPLE

FAMOUS INVENTORS FOR YOUNG PEOPLE

FAMOUS AMERICAN POETS

FAMOUS MEN OF MEDICINE

FAMOUS WOMEN OF AMERICA

FAMOUS ENGINEERS

FAMOUS OLD MASTERS OF PAINTING

FAMOUS NATURALISTS

FAMOUS MODERN AMERICAN NOVELISTS

FAMOUS BRITISH NOVELISTS

FAMOUS BRITISH POETS

FAMOUS AMERICAN STATESMEN

FAMOUS AUTHORS *for* YOUNG PEOPLE

1759

Ramon P. Coffman

Nathan G. Goodman

DODD, MEAD & COMPANY—NEW YORK

This book originally appeared under the title
"Famous Authors For Boys and Girls."

Printed in the United States of America

CONTENTS

WILLIAM SHAKESPEARE

WILLIAM SHAKESPEARE

Plays For All Time

BORN 1564—DIED 1616

AMONG ALL WRITERS in history, no other name shines more brightly than that of William Shakespeare. Some persons call him "the greatest writer who ever lived," and surely no man has been better gifted in the art of using words.

Shakespeare was born in 1564, in the month of April. Although the exact date of his birth is not on record, we know he was baptized on April 24, perhaps only a few days after his birth.

Stratford-on-Avon is the place where Shakespeare was born. To this day it is one of the charming small towns of England. Through it runs the pretty stream known as the Avon River.

Hundreds of thousands of travelers have visited Stratford-on-Avon. When you go there, you are sure to be shown the "house in which Shakespeare was born." John Shakespeare, father of the infant, was one of the leading citizens of his village. He held public offices and, when William was four, was named "high bailiff." For a time he was a merchant, dealing in gloves, and it seems that he also sold meat and wool.

During his school days William was taught writing, arithmetic and Latin. No doubt he also studied history, and he must have been deeply interested in it. In later years he was to write many plays which had to do with history.

We may picture him as a boy going to see plays in Stratford-on-Avon. In those times it was usual for plays to be given in open-air theaters. What thoughts did he have when he first saw players on a stage? We can only guess. It may be that he decided that some day he, himself, would be an actor.

There are not many records of Shakespeare's childhood and youth, but we may feel sure that he was eager for knowledge, and that he saw many things which others did not notice. In his plays he showed a wide knowledge of the outdoor world, as well as of human nature.

At the age of about thirteen, the boy had to end his studies at school. His father, while taking care of a growing family, had fallen into debt, and no longer could afford to send him to school. Will went to work, but no one knows just what he did. Possibly he became a clerk in a lawyer's office.

When Shakespeare was a young man—a very young man—he was married. He was, at the time, only eighteen years of age. His bride, Anne Hathaway, was several years older than he. Many visitors to

Stratford-on-Avon go to see "Anne Hathaway's Cottage," some little distance from the town. The guide shows visitors the fireplace beside which, it is believed, Anne and William sat in their days of courting. The very bench on which they sat, or one like it, can be seen by those who visit the old house.

At about the time he was twenty-one, Shakespeare started on the great adventure of his life. He made a journey to London. The reason he left home is not certain, but this legend has come down to us:

"There was a nobleman named Sir Thomas Lucy who owned a great deal of land near Stratford. One day Will Shakespeare went into Lucy's forest and shot a deer. He had done the same thing before, but this time he was caught. Sir Thomas Lucy did not like the Shakespeare family, and if Will had not left town he would have been punished severely."

Whether or not that story is true, we find young Shakespeare spending most of his later life away from Stratford-on-Avon. It is possible that he took his wife and children to London with him, but this is not certain. Perhaps he waited for some time before having his family come to London, or it may be that Shakespeare's parents offered their home to Mrs. Shakespeare and the little ones.

The two daughters of Shakespeare were Susanna and Judith. Hamnet, the only son, died at the age of eleven and was buried in Stratford. His name was very nearly the same as that of Hamlet, the chief character in one of the plays of Shakespeare.

During his early years in London, Shakespeare was far from being a famous writer of plays. It appears that he earned his living by small tasks performed in and around a theater. Later he was allowed to join a company of players, and after a time became one of the important actors.

Apparently Shakespeare was not content with the plays which the actors were to perform. He thought they needed to be improved, and spent some of his time writing new scenes and acts. In these efforts he proved that he had great skill.

Theaters in the time of Shakespeare had no electric lights, and most of them were not fitted even with good oil lamps. Usually the plays were given in the afternoon, more or less in the open air. An odd-looking London theater of that day was known as the "Globe." It had eight sides!

Even though there might be an open-air space for the stage, theater walls were needed to shut off the play from the eyes of the outside world. Otherwise, people might not have paid for watching the actors.

Charges were not high. One old record tells us that a person had to pay only a trifling sum to get into "the pit," very near the stage. Sometimes the pit was so closely packed that there was standing room only. Other persons bought gallery seats, for which they paid a slightly higher price.

After Shakespeare showed that he could patch up old plays and make them more popular, he was permitted to write plays of his own. The first one he wrote entirely by himself probably was "Love's Labor Lost." Later he prepared from one to three new plays each year.

As time went on, the plays became popular with English nobles and with the royal family. Shakespeare was one of three actors who were rewarded for giving a play before Queen Elizabeth. When King James I reached the throne, he honored the company of actors, and they came to be called "the King's Men."

The success Shakespeare won by his acting and by writing plays brought him a large income for those days. As soon as possible, he sent money to his father to pay off family debts, and he also bought a coat-of-arms for his father.

At the age of thirty-three, he purchased a house in Stratford-on-Avon. This house was called New Place, and is described as "one of the best in Stratford." The cost was about $250 in our money, which seems very little for a good house.

The actor and playwright did not at that time return to his home town to live. Instead he kept on with his great work. He was now one of the owners of the Globe theater, and many of his plays were acted on its stage before enthusiastic audiences.

The plays he wrote rank among the greatest of all time. They include "Hamlet," "Macbeth," "Julius Caesar," "Romeo and Juliet" and "King Lear." These plays, and others, are studied by millions of students in universities and high schools.

Besides being written in language of rare beauty, the plays of Shakespeare contain interesting stories. Here, as an example, is an outline of the story told in the play called "King Lear":

Lear, King of Britain, past the age of eighty, had decided to let others rule his kingdom. He had no son, but he called his three daughters to him and said:

"Tell me, my daughters, which of you doth love me most?"

"I love you more than words can tell," replied the eldest daughter, Princess Goneril. "You are more dear to me than the sight of my eyes. I love you no less than life itself."

Then Princess Regan spoke: "I love you even more than my sister has declared; I care for nothing else in the world except your love."

After the speeches of these two daughters, King Lear gave one-third of his kingdom to each. Then he turned to his favorite child, Cordelia, youngest of the three, and asked her what she could say.

Cordelia loved her father dearly, but she did not care to enter a contest to tell the extent of her love.

"I love you and I honor you," she stated simply, "but half of my love will go to the man I marry."

This answer made the old king angry, and he told Cordelia that he would give her share of the kingdom to her sisters.

Even though she had lost all claim to the lands of her father, Cordelia was taken in marriage by the King of France, and went to his country to live.

Before long, Lear found that he had made a mistake. Goneril and Regan were not sincere when they told of their love for him. Now that he had given away his power, he was helpless in their hands. They treated him so cruelly that, at last, he left them, preferring to brave a fierce storm than to remain in their heartless palaces.

Hearing of this, Cordelia returned to Britain with an army. Unfortunately her soldiers were defeated in battle, and she was cast into prison with her father. She died in King Lear's arms, and he learned too late how true her love had been for him.

"King Lear" is one of several tragedies written by Shakespeare. He also wrote numerous comedies and histories in play form. From the first they were very popular. They remain popular in our own day, and are played in many parts of the world, year after year.

At the age of forty-six, having written thirty-seven plays and numerous poems, the genius returned to Stratford-on-Avon. He died there in 1616, at the age of fifty-two. As a playwright and poet he ranks as a master craftsman for all time.

ROBERT BURNS

ROBERT BURNS

The Farmer Who Wrote Songs

BORN 1759—DIED 1796

SCOTLAND HAS A COUNTY called Ayrshire with an area of more than 1,100 square miles. Through it runs the Ayr River, which is only twenty miles long. The hills and valleys are dotted with farms, many of them of small size. In the low meadows and on the hillsides we may see cattle. The cows in the herds are among the best. Ayrshire cattle make up a famous breed, and may be ranked with Jerseys and Guernseys.

If we go back to 1759, we find in Ayrshire a farmer named William Burnes. He owned a small farm, on which there were a few cows. Toward the end of January in the year named, a child was born in the Burnes home. This infant was the first of seven children, and was given the name of Robert.

When Robert was only ten days old, a storm drove through the area, and the roof of the little farmhouse was damaged. Mrs. Burnes took her baby to the home of a neighbor, and he stayed there a week until the father was able to fix the roof.

Life was a struggle for the family, and the struggle grew harder as the size of the family increased. Yet the father believed in education, and tried to give his children as much of it as possible. In company with four near-by farmers, he employed a young teacher named John Murdock to give lessons to the children of the region. Among the pupils was seven-year-old Robert.

In later years Murdock reported that Robert had seemed to him a serious and thoughtful boy, but that he had no gift for music. Among all the pupils he was the least able to carry a tune.

How amazed that teacher must have been years afterward! The lad who could not carry a tune was to grow into a poet and a writer of songs. He was to give Scotland its most popular songs, and some of them were to carry across the ocean.

Through his boyhood, Robert enjoyed only snatches of education. From time to time, he studied under a teacher, but more often he read books at home. He could read only when he could be spared from the job of caring for the cows, or working in the fields.

Although Robert was not given very much schooling, he had more than his younger brothers and sisters. The father thought the eldest son should learn as much as possible, and then should teach the younger ones.

By teaching others, we, ourselves, can learn. Knowledge is not lost when it is given to others; it comes more firmly into the mind of the teacher.

Because he taught the younger children, and used much of his spare time for reading, Robert was continually gaining knowledge. The time was to arrive when, with good reason, he would be called a "well-educated man."

In the days of his boyhood and youth, life was hard for Robert's "poor-but-proud" family. At thirteen he helped thresh the grain, and at fifteen he managed much of the plowing.

Robert and his younger brother, Gilbert, were sometimes worried about their father. At the age of fifty he was keeping up the back-breaking work of the farm as he had done in his younger days.

When sixteen years old, Robert was given freedom to go to school once more. This time he studied in Kirkoswald, a town fifteen miles from his home. He learned the art of surveying, and then returned to his farm.

Kirkoswald is near the seacoast, and while Robert was there he met a sailor named Richard Brown. The sailor took an interest in the poems Robert recited to him.

"Did you make up these poems yourself?" he asked.

"Yes."

"Well, you ought to send them to a magazine. They are good."

At the age of twenty-five, Robert sorrowed over the death of his father. Now, so far as possible, he had to take the father's place.

By studying books on farming and going to fairs, he learned as much as possible about farming. Yet "one year the seed was bad, and in another the crop was scanty because of early frosts."

The young farmer in the midst of all his work kept on writing poems, and showed them to his friends. At length, when he was twenty-seven years of age, he arranged to have a printer put out a book of poetry for him. Six hundred and twelve copies were printed, and within a few months almost all of them had been sold. The author kept three copies for his family.

At this point we must note that Robert changed the spelling of his family name from "Burnes" to "Burns." He came to be known as "Robert Burns" or "Bobbie Burns."

During his young manhood, Robert Burns fell in love more than once. The names of Jean Armour, whom he married, and of "Highland Mary" have come down to us.

The real name of Highland Mary was Mary Campbell. She died within a few months after Burns' first book was published. Writing of her in his poetry, he gave her the name of Highland Mary.

Jean Armour loved Burns, and they wanted to be married. The girl's father, however, stood in the way and would not approve the marriage. Giving up hope of making a decent living from farming, and saddened by his love affair with Jean Armour, the young poet decided to leave Scotland. He would go to the New World, and take up a life anew on the island of Jamaica, a possession of Great Britain.

Then came an event which changed his plans. A friend told him that a new edition of his poems might be published at Edinburgh. This was arranged with the help of a Scottish earl, and 3,000 copies of the new volume were sold. As a reward, Burns was given a sum equal to about $2,500 in our money. We may judge the kindness of his heart from the fact that he turned over more than half of the money to his younger brothers and sisters.

The success of his book brought fame to Burns, and for several months he was the center of attention at Edinburgh. Lords and ladies gave teas and parties for him. A boy named Walter Scott was among those who saw him in the Scottish capital. In later years, when Scott himself was famous, he said he never would forget the glowing fire in the eyes of Robert Burns.

The idea of a trip to the New World was now given up, and the father of Jean Armour agreed to the marriage of his daughter to the poet. Burns rented a farm, and lived there for a time with his family. Then Burns moved to Dumfries, and was given a position as a port officer. His salary was about $450 per year.

Burns died when only thirty-seven years of age. Scotsmen grieved over his passing and spoke of him fondly as "Bobbie" Burns. He was poor at the time of his death, as during most of his life, but he left behind a rich store of songs and poetry.

"To a Mouse" and "The Cotter's Saturday Night" are among the poems of Burns. His songs include "Auld Lang Syne," "Comin' Through the Rye," and "My Heart's in the Highlands."

SIR WALTER SCOTT

SIR WALTER SCOTT

Scottish Legenas and Romances

BORN 1771—DIED 1832

THE YEAR 1826 saw the failure of a book publishing company, and this in turn brought ruin to a printing firm in Edinburgh, with debts amounting to a huge sum.

The failure of the printing firm would have been forgotten long ago if it had not been for a famous author. He was Sir Walter Scott, one of the partners.

The firm could not pay its bills, and the creditors were ready to take whatever they could get. To their surprise, Scott said to them, "Gentlemen, you shall not lose money through a firm in which I have been a partner. Give me time, and you will be paid in full!"

As to what happened after that, we shall speak later. First, however, let us go back to the youth and young manhood of Walter Scott.

He was the son of a lawyer in Edinburgh, Scotland. When only two years old, he suffered an illness which left him lame. He carried this trouble through life, but it did not make a crutch or cane necessary. He was able to take long walks, and was fond of fishing and other sports. He had few companions, and much of his childhood was spent alone. He devoted a great deal of time to reading, and became well acquainted with the legends and folklore of the Scottish people. This interest later showed itself in his stories, and poems, into which he was to weave many a tale of his native land.

During his school career, he was not among the pupils who led the class. He made poor progress in some subjects, but certain of his teachers were able to see that he had a quick mind. "I was never a dunce, nor thought to be so," he once explained, "but an incorrigibly idle little imp, who was always longing to do something else than what was enjoined him."

At the request of his father he studied law, and in 1792, at the age of twenty-one, he became a lawyer. For several years he earned his living as a lawyer, but he did not give his best to the work. He was not happy in it. Nevertheless, when he had a particular job to do, he did it. "When actually at the oar," he said, "no man could pull it harder than I, and I remember writing upwards of 120 folio pages with no interval either for food or rest."

He liked best of all to wander over the countryside, and to talk with people about old Scottish legends. As time went on, he gathered a great store of information in this field. Those who knew the young lawyer felt he ought to spend more time on law and less on legends.

As it turned out, however, the legends were to be far more important to him than the law.

Two years before he became a lawyer, Walter Scott lent his umbrella to a young woman who was about to leave a building to face a heavy shower. Her name was Margaret Belches, and the small favor led to friendship which lasted five years. Scott hoped to marry the young lady. She, however, gave her hand to another man, William Forbes.

This affair is mentioned only because it had some importance in Scott's later life. Although his close friendship with Margaret was broken, her image stayed in his mind all through his life. Another interesting point is that Forbes, many years later, proved to be a friend in time of need.

While earning his living as a lawyer, Scott wrote poems from time to time. Into his poetry he put the lore of old Scottish legends. Few persons read his early work. When he was thirty-one years old, he suffered an accident, a kick from a horse, which kept him indoors for two weeks. In this short period he wrote the first part of a long poem, "The Lay of the Last Minstrel."

After he became well again, he worked on the poem from time to time, and in three years it was published. As soon as it was off the press, it began to meet with success. The sales kept jumping from month to month.

That first success in 1805 was followed by others. The poem "Marmion" was very popular, but even its large sale was surpassed by that of "The Lady of the Lake" which appeared in 1810. Its publication made certain Scott's fame as a writer. Millions of boys and girls have read "The Lady of the Lake" in school.

In the year 1811 he bought a large tract of land beside the Tweed River, and there built what he at first called a "cottage." Later he kept building new rooms and new wings until the structure became a great mansion, large enough to hold scores of relatives and friends who came to visit him on special occasions. In this big house it was his custom to write two or three hours before breakfast. Part of the day was spent in riding, shooting, looking after favorite dogs and horses, and entertaining guests, but the author found time for further writing.

Before Scott wrote "The Lady of the Lake" and his other famous poems, he was married to Charlotte Carpenter, who proved a helpful wife. In their early years of marriage, they lived in a small cottage, but later they moved into what Scott called his "fairy palace," the huge building with plenty of land in every direction.

It was in 1814, while searching for some fishing-tackle, that he stumbled upon an old manuscript which he had written years before. For three weeks he worked furiously over this unfinished story until it was ready, and then purposely had it published without his name. Although, for some time, readers did not know the name of the author, they welcomed the book. It was a novel, "Waverley," a story about Scotland in 1745. Its immediate success caused Scott to make an important decision. In the future his pen would be turned to historical novels. He wrote "The Heart of Midlothian," "Guy Mannering," "Kenilworth" and "The Talisman."

"The Talisman," a novel drawn from history, deals with one of the Crusades of the Middle Ages. Richard-the-Lion-Hearted and Saladin are characters in the book.

Richard and Saladin led opposing armies, but it seems they admired each other a great deal and exchanged letters. Tales have been told of friendly meetings between them. Although these stories are interesting, they are not to be taken as completely true history.

Scott's most widely read novel is "Ivanhoe," which is part of the course in English in many high schools. The manners and customs of the Age of Chivalry are packed into this exciting story. King Richard-the-Lion-Hearted, Robin Hood and the jolly Friar Tuck appear in it. The heroine, Scott's favorite, is a beautiful and generous Jewish maiden named Rebecca. Her character is drawn from real life. The original Rebecca lived in Philadelphia and devoted her life to deeds of charity. It was Washington Irving who told Scott about her. He gave such a glowing account of her beauty and goodness that Scott decided to make her the heroine of his next novel, which turned out to be "Ivanhoe."

Other novels by Scott were built around different periods in history. He showed special interest in the Middle Ages, and wrote a great deal about knights and castles and fair ladies. He found more excitement in the life of the past than in the everyday world of his own day. Of his twenty-six novels, written in seventeen years, sixteen deal with men and events in Scottish history; six are based on English history; and four are stories of places beyond British borders.

Scott's novels were not meant to be exactly true, but they were based on his study of old customs. As we read them, the life of bygone times seems to come back to us. The volumes were the "best sellers" of their day. They were read all over Great Britain, and their fame spread abroad. As a reward for his great skill, he was made a knight, and he is best known today as "Sir Walter Scott."

Sir Walter Scott lived in the time of Napoleon Bonaparte. Napoleon was the terror of his time. Leading armies from place to place, he conquered one country after another, and Europe was drenched in blood.

One nation, above all others, stood out against Napoleon. Great Britain would not bow before his cannon. In the end Napoleon was brought down, losing the Battle of the Nations and the Battle of Waterloo.

Some persons think of a man who leads armies of conquest as "great." He may cause the death of millions of human beings, but if he wins his way, those persons class him as "a great man." Napoleon's memory lives to this day, but so does the memory of a man whose work was with the pen. Sir Walter Scott lives in a very real way in his poems and novels.

Perhaps he did his best work when writing about the people and places in the history of Scotland in the seventeenth and eighteenth centuries. His stories of other countries and earlier periods are also celebrated. Not only was Scott a great writer; he was also a great and honorable man. This he showed clearly when the fearful blow came to his personal fortune. When his printing firm failed, he shared in the debt of $600,000. His partners could pay nothing, so he shouldered the debt alone, telling the creditors that if they would wait, he would pay the money.

It was at this time that he did the hardest work of his life. Quickly he wrote new novels, and his payments for them were immediately used to pay the huge debt. In two years he paid almost $200,000.

Overwork led to illness, and the illness was so severe that he could write no more. In his last years, the thought of "payment in full" seems to have been in his mind almost constantly. Shortly before death came, he said to a friend at his bedside: "Be a good man. Nothing else will give you any comfort when you come to lie here."

In 1832, at the age of sixty-one, he died at his home near the Tweed River. Although he had not completed payment of the debt, the balance was cleared with money obtained through the sale of copyrights for his books. Thus the aim of his later life was fully accomplished, and the whole world grew richer because of the great books produced by Sir Walter Scott.

WASHINGTON IRVING

WASHINGTON IRVING

Rip Van Winkle's Long Nap

BORN 1783—DIED 1859

IN PRESENT-DAY FAMILIES there are usually from one to four children, but when Washington Irving was born—back in the year 1783—large families were common. There were eleven children in the Irving family, but it was looked upon as merely "middle-sized."

The youngest of the eleven children was named "Washington," in honor of George Washington. Several years later, after he had become President, Washington was in a New York store when a young woman stepped to his side and said, "Please, your honor, here's a boy who was named after you." The young woman was a maid in the Irving household. The President looked down and saw little Washington Irving. Patting him on the head, he spoke friendly words to the little fellow.

When the boy grew into manhood, he made a journey to France.

1759

At a French seaport, he boarded a vessel flying the American flag to go to the island of Sicily in the Mediterranean.

In those days there was danger of falling into the hands of pirates while sailing the Mediterranean Sea. Young Irving's vessel was halted by a band of pirates, and they shouted orders in a language which the captain could not understand. At length Irving, who knew how to speak French, was sent aboard the pirate ship. There he talked to "men with rough beards and fierce black eyes." They told him that they wanted a supply of food.

After being given the food, the pirates let the American vessel go on its way, without harming anyone aboard. Irving was glad when he safely set foot on Sicily. Later he spent several months in Italy. During a visit to Mt. Vesuvius, he saw the volcano sending forth flame and smoke; he walked so close to the crater that he was nearly choked by the vapors.

Returning to New York, he joined one of his brothers and a friend in starting a magazine. The magazine was fairly successful, but was allowed to "die" after twenty issues had been published. Later, however, great success in the writing world was won by young Washington Irving.

A December day in the year 1809 saw two new volumes appear on the counters of book shops in New York City. They were a two-volume "History of New York."

The name of the author was given as "Diedrich Knickerbocker." It was said that he belonged to an old Dutch family, but that he had lately disappeared. The history was supposed to have been published to pay debts which Knickerbocker had left behind him.

As December passed, more and more people read and talked about this "History of New York." It told a great deal about early Dutch settlers. Some members of the rich Dutch families in the city felt that the book poked fun at their ancestors, and said they would tell their friends not to buy it.

The secret at last came out, but in the meantime Irving enjoyed hugely the widespread talk about Knickerbocker and the history. The fame of this work soon spread abroad, and Sir Walter Scott read it. In a letter, Scott said that he and his friends were so much amused that their "sides were sore with laughing."

Many famous writers of humor have had deep sorrow in their own lives. In the years just before the history was published, such sorrow came to Irving. He suffered the loss of his father, of his favorite sister, and of Matilda Hoffman.

Matilda Hoffman was the young woman he had planned to marry. In his mind she was the most charming person in the world. Her death filled him with grief, and instead of rising beyond it he kept it heavily in his heart. During his long life he remained a bachelor. If his mind turned to romance, he thought of the girl who had died "in the sweet beauty of her youth."

Yet Irving spoke little of his sorrow to those he met in his travels through life. His friends and relatives found in him good nature and kindness, and were happy to be in his company.

Sailing to England, he spent years there and on the continent of Europe. Day after day he wrote in his "Sketch Book," and sent his writings back to the United States. The stories which now came from Irving's pen were among the best of his life. They included "Rip Van Winkle" and "The Legend of Sleepy Hollow," a ghostly tale about a poor schoolmaster and the headless horseman who haunted the neighborhood.

Millions of boys and girls have read "Rip Van Winkle," the story of a man who went to sleep for twenty years. Rip found the world very different after he woke up! In the meantime the War for Independence had been fought and won.

When Washington Irving crossed the Atlantic in 1815, he expected to stay abroad only a few months. As it turned out, he spent the next seventeen years in Great Britain and on the continent of Europe!

As a boy Irving had sailed up and down the Hudson River, and had enjoyed the scenery. Best of all he had liked the Catskill Mountains, which shelter the valley of Sleepy Hollow. The memory of the Catskills stayed with him while he was in Europe, and he wove stories about them. His tale of Rip Van Winkle and his long sleep in the Catskills was published in the United States during this time. Reports of its widespread success were carried to him by letter, and cheered him greatly.

At the age of forty-three Irving went to Spain, and stayed there for six years. They were busy years; he often arose at six o'clock in the morning to start his writing. The first book he wrote while in Spain was "The Life of Columbus." It was followed by several other volumes, one of them being "The Alhambra."

While in Madrid, the Spanish capital, Irving was visited by a twenty-year-old American who was making a tour of Europe. The young man was later to become widely known. He was Henry Wadsworth Longfellow. Writing to his father, Longfellow said that Irving was "one of those men who put you at ease with them in a moment."

Men who give their lives to writing are seldom offered political offices. Yet Irving, after his return to the United States, was asked to become American minister to Spain. He accepted, and went back to Spain for a period of four years.

Once more in the United States, Washington Irving made his home close to Sleepy Hollow, in a dwelling called "Sunnyside." There he went on with his writing, and in the last five years of his life wrote a biography of George Washington. During the year in which he died, the final volume of the biography was finished. The hero about whom he wrote was the man for whom he had been named.

At one time Irving started to write the story of the Spanish invasion of Mexico, but learned that a young author named Prescott had the same plan in mind. So he gave up the story, saying, "I will leave the field open for Mr. Prescott."

Washington Irving was seventy-six years old at the time of his death. His life had been rich in its gifts to the world, and to the end he was kind to those about him.

THOMAS CARLYLE

THOMAS CARLYLE

A Stormy Life

BORN 1795—DIED 1881

STORIES ABOUT BABIES often are not quite true to fact. With the passing of years a child may be told about things which he did as a baby, but the person who tells him may not remember the events just as they happened.

Whether it is true or not, here is a story about Baby Thomas Carlyle:

Up to the age of eleven months, the baby had not spoken a word, not even "dada" or "mamma." Then came a day when a small boy in the house began to cry, and from the cradle came a question, "What ails wee Jack?"

Although it cannot be said for certain that little Tom started his talking with a whole sentence, it might be so. Now and then an infant amazes older persons by one kind of skill or another.

Thomas Carlyle was born in Scotland in 1795. His father was a mason and, later in his life, a farmer. The family grew until there were nine children.

Little money was to be found in the Carlyle household. Yet the father cared enough about education to send his children to school. Tom at first studied in the village school, then was sent to a grammar-school in a near-by town. He liked arithmetic.

Both schools cost the family money; it was the custom almost everywhere in those days to charge the pupils fees. Therefore, many children were unable to attend school.

Thomas was always troubled by his own nature. He was an earnest lad, but he had a violent temper. His mother knew the dangers into which a fit of temper might lead him. She, therefore, made him promise never to hit back no matter what the reason. The boys soon knew that they could torment Tom as much as they pleased and so they did. After a time the bullying became more than the lonely boy could bear. In spite of the promise he had kept so faithfully, Thomas finally hit back at one of the biggest of his tormentors with such hard blows that, afterwards, the boys respected him. These were not very happy days for the lad.

Before his fourteenth birthday, the boy was ready to enter college. The distance to Edinburgh was more than seventy miles, and how do you suppose he got there? He walked!

The journey was made in company with another youth. There was little in the way of "hitch-hiking" in those times, but the young travelers were taken aboard a cart for a few miles. They reached Edinburgh in three days.

It was the plan of Thomas Carlyle to study to become a minister. He little knew that he would give his life to writing instead, and would become a famous author.

While he was a student at the University of Edinburgh, Carlyle's food was made up largely of things sent to him from his home. Parcels containing "porridge, ham, salt, butter and potatoes" came to him from the farm.

Although he had to eat to live, Carlyle's mind was for the most part on other things. He was studying logic, moral philosophy, Latin and Greek, and had a strong desire to master completely each of his subjects.

Although he studied for five years at the university, Carlyle did not complete his course. He gave up the idea of being a minister. Even in his grammar-school days he had received excellent marks in arithmetic, so he made up his mind to teach mathematics. He did not enjoy teaching, however, and soon gave that up, too. Then he studied law for a short time.

Finally, Carlyle found a little encouragement. He wrote some articles for an encyclopedia and received money for them. It was not a large sum, but it was enough to set him on the right path. He would be a writer.

He worked harder and harder and, besides, was forced to fight against illness. By the time his story of the life of Schiller, the German poet, was published, he began to feel that in time he would be successful. He was then thirty years of age.

A few years later, he moved to a quiet, restful farm in Scotland away from the noise of the city streets. His wife, Jane, a beautiful and capable young woman, did all in her power to help and comfort her husband. She knew him to be a genius, but he was so often ill and in low spirits that her life was not a very happy one.

During the years that Carlyle was teaching mathematics, he found a good friend, who helped to change his life. This man, a schoolmaster, led his younger friend to take an interest in history. Years later, Carlyle was to write a world-famous history book, but he had to write it twice!

If you labored for a long time in writing a book, and then found your manuscript gone—burned up—how would you feel about it?

That happened to Thomas Carlyle. He worked ever so hard on a volume to be called "The French Revolution" and felt that he had done a good piece of work. He hoped it would prove a better success than anything he had written before.

To his home came a friend, John Stuart Mill. This friend was also a writer, and was destined to win fame in his own field. He was much interested in the work of Carlyle, who was ten years older than himself.

"You may take the manuscript along with you and read it," Carlyle said to Mill.

So it came about that the book started on its journey toward misfortune. Mill was so pleased with it that he lent the manuscript to a friend, and she put it aside for a time.

A servant was starting a fire and was looking about for some paper to kindle it. She laid hands on the manuscript supposing it to be something which no one wanted. Up in smoke it went—lost to the world! There are times when greatness is proved by meeting misfortune bravely. Both Mill and Carlyle did so in this case.

Heart-broken, Mill went to tell the story to his friend, and handed him a sum equal in our money to $1,000.

Carlyle was poor, and had been so all his life. He did not want to take the money, but at last said, "I will take half of it, and will use it to pay my expenses while I am writing the book over again."

Once more he set to work and wrote about the French Revolution, and this time the manuscript found its way to the publisher. To his wife he said, "This book has come from my heart."

When the volume was printed, it proved a real success. Carlyle's fame spread far and wide. His words were read on both sides of the Atlantic.

So it came about that a lost book was given back to the world. Because Carlyle would not let a blow put him down, he was able to produce a masterpiece. In later years he was to write other important books, but "The French Revolution" marked the beginning of his great success.

People often disagreed with the things Carlyle wrote. A series of articles in one of the magazines of the day was severely criticized by many readers. Others thought the articles full of wit and humor. Finally, they were published in a book which became one of the famous pieces of literature. It is called "Sartor Resartus." The title means "The Tailor Patched Again" and the book tries to show what mankind really is. In this book he tells a great deal about himself.

The Carlyles spent some of their later years in London. Their house in a quiet London street was kept as a memorial after Thomas Carlyle's death.

NATHANIEL HAWTHORNE

NATHANIEL HAWTHORNE

Stories of New England

BORN 1804—DIED 1864

IF YOU HAD PAID a visit to a certain home in Salem, Massachusetts, in 1827, you would have found a rather strange situation there. Three members of the family were in the habit of "keeping to their rooms." The fourth person in the family, a young woman, paid them visits from time to time, but not very many, since the others were not very anxious for company.

It was the Hathorne family, the name of which later was changed to "Hawthorne" by its only male member. Mrs. Hathorne had taken to her own room shortly after the death of her husband, nineteen years before. One of her daughters, probably in imitation, had done the same thing shortly after she grew up. Her only son, too, after coming back from college, had chosen a room for himself and stayed in it most of the time, often eating his meals there. The meals, we are told, were placed beside his door and when he felt hungry he opened the door and took them inside.

The son, Nathaniel, perhaps had the best reason for keeping away from the family and the rest of the world. He was trying to be a writer. He had reached the age of twenty-three, and felt that it was time to work seriously on magazine articles and books. While studying at Bowdoin, a small college in Maine, he had made a few friends, one of them the poet Longfellow. For the most part, however, he had lived inside his own mind.

After finishing a book, which he called "Seven Tales of My Native Land," Nathaniel took it, or mailed it, to seventeen book publishing companies, but each one refused to accept it. Then he wrote another book, a novel called "Fanshawe." This he was able to have printed by paying the cost from his own pocket. There were not many copies sold, however, and the young author marked it down as a failure.

From time to time, as the years went by, a magazine would accept an article or story from Hawthorne's pen. This gave him hope that sooner or later he might make a success of his writing. Yet with all his skill in handling words, he lacked something as an author. He knew too little of the actual world.

What would have been his fate if an interested visitor had not knocked at the door of his home it is hard to say. As it was, a young woman called at the house one day to see the writer of a piece called "The Gentle Boy." She believed it had been written by one of Hawthorne's sisters. When told who really had written the story, she said she admired it very much and would like the author and his sisters to call at her home.

Thus, Nathaniel Hawthorne, "dragged away" as it seemed to him, visited the Peabody home. It was here that he met the sister of the young woman who had invited him to come to see her. The sister was named Sophia, and when Hawthorne caught sight of her, he had a hard time taking his eyes from her face. Sophia Peabody at that time was an invalid, and could not leave her own home, but her face seemed noble and beautiful to the writer who had kept himself so well penned away from the world. There was in his mind a memory of the period in his boyhood when, after injuring his leg, he had been confined to his house for several years. The remembrance of those lonely days gave him a special sympathy for the young woman on whose face he now gazed.

That visit opened the door to a friendship which grew as the months passed. After two years Nathaniel and Sophia became engaged, but Sophia said that the engagement must not turn into marriage until her health became so good that she no longer would be an invalid. Perhaps it was a deep love which proved better than the doctor's medicine; at any rate, three years after the engagement, she was well and the marriage took place.

Meanwhile Nathaniel Hawthorne had decided to go out into the real world, and to work at tasks other than writing. He obtained a place, at a salary of one hundred dollars a month, at the Boston Custom House where he labored hard, weighing coal and other goods which sea-going vessels brought into the port. That was in 1839, the same year in which he became engaged to Miss Peabody. While he was away from Salem, he wrote many letters to his fiancée, letters which told how tenderly he cared for her and how much she meant in his life.

Fourteen months later, Hawthorne gave up his work at the port, but soon thereafter entered upon farm work. He joined Charles A. Dana and others in forming a little village called "Brook Farm." All persons in the village did their share of work. Hawthorne often got up at four o'clock in the morning to start plowing, hoeing or reaping. Although he enjoyed talking with the brilliant men and women who gathered in the tiny settlement, he decided that he would not live there when the day of his marriage came.

About the time he was married, Hawthorne obtained a position at the Salem Custom House, and there he lived with his beloved wife in a house known as "The Old Manse." Some years before, another great writer, Ralph Waldo Emerson, had lived in the same house.

By this time, Hawthorne had written several new books, and these had enjoyed a slight success with the public. Yet he still thought of himself as "the world's least-read author." In his free time he kept on with his writing, but sent very little of it to publishers. Nevertheless, his four years at "The Old Manse" were good ones; the sweet nature of his wife gave a happiness of spirit to him which he had not known before.

With a change of government, Hawthorne lost his post at the Cus-

tom House and moved to a different house in Salem. There he was under the need of making his writing help to pay family expenses. The Hawthornes had three children to provide for. One day a publisher, James Fields, came to see him and found him "in a chamber above the sitting room, hovering near a stove." The author seemed very down-hearted.

"Now," said Fields, "is the time for you to publish a new book!"

"Nonsense!" replied Hawthorne. "Who would risk publishing a book for me when Monroe and Company have been so many years trying to sell a small edition of my 'Twice-told Tales'?"

"I am ready to publish a new book of yours!" said the publisher. "What manuscript do you have ready?"

Hawthorne protested that he had nothing which deserved to be printed. However, he at last handed over a roll of manuscript. Fields thanked him and hurried to catch his train to Boston. On the way there, he read the story which was to be printed under the title of "The Scarlet Letter."

When "The Scarlet Letter" was published, it proved a greater success than Hawthorne had ever imagined. Five thousand copies were sold in ten days, a remarkable record at that time. The new book spread his fame far and wide. Readers in England, as well as in the United States, praised it as a work of art.

Hawthorne was forty-six years old when "The Scarlet Letter" was published. This volume was followed within the next few years by "The House of Seven Gables," "The Blithedale Romance" and

"Tanglewood Tales." These books also met a friendly reception, and did much to place Hawthorne in the front rank of American authors.

In his "Tanglewood Tales" Hawthorne retold for his own children the stories from Greek mythology that all boys and girls love to hear.

Among the few friends Hawthorne had made while at college was one who later became President of the United States. This man was Franklin Pierce. Shortly after taking office, Pierce appointed Hawthorne as American Consul at Liverpool. Sailing for England in 1853 with his family, he spent the next four years abroad. He was especially happy to give his wife and children the experience of living for a time in another country.

Leaving England, the Hawthorne family crossed to the continent of Europe and spent a year in Italy. Then a return journey was made to England, and for a year the author worked there on a new book, "The Marble Faun."

Returning to America, Hawthorne spent the last few years of his life chiefly at Concord, Massachusetts. About the middle of May, 1864, he set out on a tour of New England in the company of his good friend, Franklin Pierce. He was not in very good health and, within five days after the start of the trip, Hawthorne died at Plymouth, New Hampshire. He left behind him many fine pieces of writing, including "note-books" of his travels in Europe, which were published after his death. His son, Julian, followed in his father's footsteps and he, too, became a writer.

HANS CHRISTIAN ANDERSEN

HANS CHRISTIAN ANDERSEN

Fairy Tales That Live Today

BORN 1805—DIED 1875

THERE WAS A DINNER party going on at the home of a wealthy man in Denmark. Although he was of Italian birth, the wealthy man was director of the Academy of Music in Copenhagen. It was the year 1819.

Up to the door of the house stepped a fourteen-year-old boy. He had come to Copenhagen from another part of Denmark, and had been in the capital city only a few weeks. The small sum of money which he had brought with him had almost run out, and he had decided to make a last effort to "win his fortune" before going back to his native village.

The woman who served as housekeeper for the mansion opened the door, and asked what the boy wanted.

"I would like to see Mr. Siboni," he replied.

"What is your name and what do you want to see him about?"

"I am Hans Andersen, and I come from the village of Odense. People in Odense say that I have a fine voice, and I came here to sing or act on the stage. My father is dead. He was a shoemaker by trade. My mother wanted me to be a tailor, but I coaxed her to let me come to this city and try my fortune. Now I have hardly a bit of money left. Do you think Mr. Siboni would listen to me while I sing a few songs for him?"

"I shall ask him about it," said the housekeeper kindly.

For many minutes the boy was left waiting. Then Mr. Siboni came from the dining room, followed by his guests, and said, "We should like to hear you sing."

Hans was quick to break into a song, and after he finished that, he recited poems for the men who were listening.

"I shall help you train your voice," said Siboni at length.

The boy heard the pleasant words, and turned to leave the house. In the hallway, the housekeeper patted him on the cheek and said, "Tomorrow you must go to see Professor Weyse, and he will do something for you."

The next day the boy paid a visit to the professor and was given a sum of money amounting to several dollars. Quickly he wrote a letter to his mother, telling her of his good fortune.

Shortly afterward, Siboni told the boy he could come to his home to live, and there for six months he was a guest and pupil. The training went on for six months, but toward the end of that period Hans found that something had happened to his vocal chords, something which took away the clear notes which he had been able to produce before. Siboni also noticed the change, and said, "I am sorry that it is unlikely that you will become a good singer. You had best go back to Odense and learn a trade."

The advice no doubt was good, but Hans felt as though the world had broken around him. If he returned to Odense, he thought, all hope of his making a mark in the world would be gone.

At this point Hans decided to write a letter to a poet named Guldberg, who lived in a suburb of Copenhagen. This poet was a brother of a friendly army colonel who lived in Odense. Soon after writing the letter, the boy went to the poet's home.

Having heard his visitor's story, Guldberg decided to help him as much as possible. He had noticed that the letter was filled with misspelled words, and thought that the best thing to do was to give Hans lessons in the Danish language. He also told Hans that he had recently published a small book, and would give him the profits from the sale of it. True to his word, Guldberg turned over to Hans enough money to pay his board and room for many weeks. He also gave him the much-needed lessons in grammar. He, furthermore, persuaded a friend to teach Hans Latin twice a week.

Before many years went by, Hans gave up his Latin lessons. His real hope now was that he might find a place as an actor on the stage, and he had heard that an actor could get along very well without knowing Latin. As often as he could, he went to the theater, and soon became slightly acquainted with some of the actors. Yet, despite all his efforts, he could make no progress in getting work in a theater.

Without completely losing heart, the youth turned his time to the writing of a play. In two weeks he finished what he called "a tragedy" and it was shown to people in the theatrical world. Six weeks later it was sent back to him with the statement that he needed a better education before he could hope to write a play.

Again Hans found his hopes dashed, but he did not give up. By this time he was eighteen years of age and he firmly believed that he would, by some miracle, win success. It was the director of the Royal Theater, a man named Jonas Collin, who put him on the path to better luck. Collin recommended him to the Danish king, Frederick VI, and the king granted him a pension, which he could use for further education.

Now it was possible for Hans Christian Andersen to attend school in earnest. He was placed, however, in a class with boys much younger and smaller than himself. He worked hard on his studies, and after much struggle was rewarded with good marks. In that way he made up, to a large degree, for the scanty education of his childhood.

From time to time young Andersen wrote poetry, and at about the time of his twenty-fifth birthday a book of his poems was printed. One poem, "The Dying Child," was so good that it helped to build a little fame for the author. Yet he still was far from winning a high place in the field of writing.

When Andersen was twenty-eight years old, the Danish king once more helped him. This time he was granted a pension to use while traveling, and he made a journey through Germany and France to Switzerland and Italy. Later he traveled in Sweden. Along the way, he wrote travel books. He also wrote novels which were based, in part, on his adventures. The title of one of his most popular novels was "Only a Fiddler."

Some people praised Andersen's books, but others said they did not amount to a great deal. The author read the words of the newspaper and magazine critics with special attention and was downhearted when anyone spoke against his books.

Andersen often spent many hours with boys and girls, whose company he enjoyed. By this time there were various homes in Copenhagen where he was a welcome guest, and in those homes the children liked to have him tell stories. At length he wrote down several stories which the children had enjoyed, and they were published under the title of "Stories Told for Children." The author, however, was doubtful that a man who was working to be a great novelist should spend any of his time writing such books.

The first volume of children's stories was composed of tales which Andersen himself had heard when he was a child. So many copies were sold that publishers asked him for another book of the same kind for the next Christmas season. This new volume also found a good sale, and he was asked to write still another. So it came about that he kept on writing more and more stories for children. As time passed, he found that, when he made up fairy tales from his own mind instead of telling those he had heard as a child, they were even more popular with the public.

In that way, quite by chance, Andersen found his field. As a writer of fairy tales, he was a master and won the praise of people not only in Denmark but in other countries as well. His stories were translated into German, Swedish, English and other languages, and his fame kept growing until it became world-wide. The well-loved stories which he produced, and which are widely read to the present time, include "The Fir Tree," "The Constant Tin Soldier" and "The Ugly Duckling."

Happy were the thoughts of the author as his books kept on selling widely, and as honor was shown him in many lands. The poor shoemaker's son, who had come to Copenhagen to make his fortune, was now hailed as one of the great writers of his time. He had met bitter trials, and failure after failure. Yet, as he looked back, he saw that his youth and young manhood had contained much besides bitter trials. In the years when he was trying to find himself, he had met with kind people, and they had helped him time and time again. It was almost beyond belief that some of them could have had the good will to take in a stranger and do so much for him in the big city. This experience of the poor boy who found good fortune, of the stranger to whom doors were opened, really formed in his mind a basis for his fairy tales. Although he invented stories, there was something of truth in them—truth from his own life.

Andersen, himself, knew how to be kind to others. One day he heard that a young lady from Sweden, named Jenny Lind, had come to Copenhagen. She was a singer, as he had heard, but she never had sung to the public outside of Sweden, her native land. Feeling that he might give her a word of welcome, he called on her, and this visit led to an acquaintance which helped Jenny Lind become known outside her own country. In 1843 Andersen persuaded her to give a concert in Copenhagen, and it proved so successful that she became "the toast of the town." Danish students formed a torchlight parade and surrounded the house where she was staying to give her a serenade. Pleased by this first foreign excursion, Jenny Lind soon afterward gave concerts in other parts of Europe, and at length visited the United States where there never were enough seats for the people who wanted to hear her sing.

On his seventieth birthday, Hans Christian Andersen was given a book which contained one of his fairy stories printed in Danish and in fourteen foreign languages. At the same time he was given the Grand Cross of the Dannebrog Order. Upon his death, he was mourned by people in many parts of the world, most of whom knew him only through his delightful stories for children.

HENRY WADSWORTH LONGFELLOW

HENRY WADSWORTH LONGFELLOW

The Children's Poet

BORN 1807—DIED 1882

IN THE YEAR 1820 a newspaper in Portland, Maine, published a short poem by a thirteen-year-old boy who signed himself "H." The lad who wrote the poem was Henry Wadsworth Longfellow.

Henry was born in Portland in 1807 in a house near the fine harbor which that city possesses. His grandfather, General Wadsworth, had fought in the American Revolution, and in later life lived in the backwoods of Maine in pioneer fashion. The Longfellow children spent many of their summers on the General's frontier farm. Henry was fond of toddling around at his grandfather's heels, and sometimes helped him bring the cows in from pasture. The little fellow listened with wide-open eyes to the tales of war which the old General told him, and for a long time Henry felt sure he would follow the same profession.

When he was only three years old, Henry began to learn his ABC's. In company with his older brother, Stephen, he attended school, and as the years went by he became known as a very bright pupil, fond of his studies. He was ready for college when only fourteen years of age.

Mr. Longfellow sent his sons to a new college, Bowdoin, only thirty miles away. A stagecoach pitched them from side to side for five hours as it carried them over the bumpy road from Portland to Brunswick. One of Henry's classmates was Nathaniel Hawthorne, who later was to be a writer of great note.

Young Longfellow did so well in his college studies that he was offered a position as teacher of foreign languages at Bowdoin. He liked the idea, and decided to go abroad to learn more about languages. Aboard a slow-moving sailing-vessel, he traveled to Europe and spent three years in France, Spain and Italy. He was twenty-two when he returned to the United States, and started his work of teaching at Bowdoin.

Longfellow was married to a playmate of his childhood, Mary Potter. A few years later he went to Europe again. This time he visited England, Sweden, Denmark, Germany and Holland. His wife traveled with him, and their tour was happy until they reached Holland. In that little country, Mrs. Longfellow fell sick and died. In one of his later poems, Longfellow wrote: "Into each life some rain must fall." The young professor bore his loss bravely, in the same way he was to meet other deep sorrows of his life.

After his second European trip, Longfellow became a professor at Harvard and taught foreign languages there for seventeen years. He was a favorite among the students, and worked to give them a true picture of the life and spirit of the nations of Europe. In his spare moments he wrote poems. At first his writing seemed little more than a hobby, but later he gave a great deal of his time to it.

While teaching at Harvard, Longfellow married again. His second wife was Frances Appleton, and they lived in an old, but well-built, house in Cambridge, Massachusetts. It was known as "Craigie House." Not far away was a large chestnut tree. When the poet went for a walk, he often passed the tree and sometimes stopped to watch a blacksmith, whose shop was shaded by the branches of the fine, old tree. By and by he wrote a poem about the tree and the blacksmith. It has been read by millions of children, and has been learned by heart by many of them.

"The Village Blacksmith" starts with the words:

> Under the spreading chestnut tree,
> The village smithy stands.

It is a short poem, with only eight stanzas and forty-eight lines, but there is a swing to it which has made it popular. In one of the stanzas, we read:

> And children coming home from school
> Look in at the open door·

They love to see the flaming forge,
And hear the bellows roar,
And catch the burning sparks that fly
Like chaff from a threshing floor.

Another of Longfellow's poems sprang from a place even closer to him—from his own home, and his three little daughters. He called it "The Children's Hour." It runs, in part, like this:

I hear in the chamber above me
The patter of little feet,
The sound of a door that is opened
And voices soft and sweet.

From my study, I see in the lamplight,
Descending the broad hall stair,
Grave Alice and laughing Allegra,
And Edith with golden hair.

A whisper and then a silence:
Yet I know by their merry eyes
They are plotting and planning together
To take me by surprise.

Among the longer poems of Longfellow is one called "The Song of Hiawatha." It was woven out of Indian legends, and contains more than four thousand lines. In large part it was based on notes about Indian life made by a man named Schoolcraft, who had visited a number of tribes in their own villages. Longfellow, however, seems to have obtained part of the material from an Ojibway chief who came to Cambridge and talked with the poet in his home.

Nathaniel Hawthorne, Longfellow's old college classmate, had remained his good friend. One day they had dinner together, and with them sat a clergyman, Reverend H. L. Conolly.

"It is strange," said the clergyman, turning to Hawthorne, "that you have not written a romance about the Acadian tale which I told you some time ago."

Longfellow asked what tale he was speaking about, and in return heard this story:

"A French Canadian told me about a young couple in Acadia who were to be married on a certain day. The wedding was hardly over when the men of the province were seized and sent to different parts of New England. One of those forced to leave was the new bridegroom. His bride later followed him to New England, but could not find him. Year after year she searched—and then, at last, she located him, as he lay dying."

Since Hawthorne did not care to use the tale as the plot for a novel, Longfellow asked whether he might use it for a poem. "Certainly," replied Hawthorne, and so it came about that Longfellow wrote "Evangeline," which ranks among the best of his poems. He finished writing it on his fortieth birthday.

Some years later, Longfellow wrote another long poem, "The Courtship of Miles Standish." For a time he planned to call this poem "Priscilla," but changed the title when he was about half-way through writing it. "The Courtship of Miles Standish" deals with the Pilgrims at Plymouth, and contains a line often quoted, "Why don't you speak for yourself, John?" The question, we are told, was asked during a visit which John Alden made to Priscilla. Serving as a messenger from Captain Miles Standish, John asked Priscilla whether she would marry Standish. This was hard for John to do, since he, himself, was fond of the Pilgrim maiden. In the end, Priscilla married the messenger! John Alden and Priscilla were among the great-great-great grandparents of Longfellow.

Henry Wadsworth Longfellow lived to the age of seventy-five. Three years before his death a group of school children came to visit him. With them, they brought a present—an armchair made from wood of the "spreading chestnut tree" which the beloved poet had made famous.

CHARLES DICKENS

CHARLES DICKENS

Factory Boy to Novelist

BORN 1812—DIED 1870

ON THE SOUTHERN coast of England is Portsmouth, an important seaport with a population of more than a quarter of a million people. In the year 1819, a suburb of Portsmouth was the home of a clerk named John Dickens. Mr. Dickens was at that time earning enough money to take care of his growing family comfortably. Among his children was a seven-year-old boy, Charles. He had already learned from his mother a little about the art of reading.

In those days schools were not free. If parents knew how to read and write, they might teach their children. If they could afford to pay for teaching, the children might be sent to school. By and by, little Charles was entered in a school. He took an interest in his studies, and made better progress than most of the other pupils. He was encouraged, and his parents were pleased.

A year later Mr. Dickens lost his job. He then moved to London and tried to earn a living in different work, but had little success. Things went from bad to worse, with debts piling up. Then came the dreadful time when officers of the law put him under arrest and he was taken to prison, to stay until his debts were paid. This was a hard blow to the whole family

With his father in prison, eleven-year-old Charles was set to work. A distant cousin owned a factory in London in which shoe blacking was made. Here the lad worked day after day, earning six shillings a week, or about a dollar and a half in our money. He was provided with a room in a lodging house, but had to buy his food with his own money from his small salary. For breakfast, he usually had "a penny cottage loaf and a pennyworth of milk." In the evening he ate bread and cheese in his own room. Between those meals, he bought coffee, sweets and "a slice of pudding" when he had money to spare.

At the blacking factory Charles covered jars of blacking first with oil paper and then with blue paper. He pasted printed labels over the blue paper. Thousands of jars passed through his tired hands in a few months. There were other boys at the factory, half a dozen of them. One was Bob Fagin, an orphan, who proved quite friendly. Later Bob was to be named as a character in a book called "Oliver Twist."

Today there is a common rule of law which says no one shall be put in prison for debt. This is now true in Great Britain, as in other modern countries, but when Charles Dickens was a boy, it was not.

Charles suffered constantly over the thought of his father's being in prison. He kept his father's ill fortune a secret from the boys who worked with him at the blacking factory.

According to this old law a man in prison for debts had to stay there until his debts were paid. This seems odd to us. We may ask, "How could he ever pay what he owed if he did not work?" For many men, there was no good answer to this question. In the case of others it sometimes happened that friends or relatives supplied the needed money. To John Dickens, the answer luckily came in the form of a little fortune, something like $2,000, which was left to him by the will of a relative.

Out of prison came Mr. Dickens, and out of the blacking factory came Charles. His father, a good-hearted man, sent the boy to school again. The school was known as Wellington House Academy. The headmaster, a Welshman named Jones, seems to have been harsh in his treatment of the boys. Perhaps he had reason to be harsh. Many of the boys in his school spent much of their time discovering new forms of mischief. They brought white mice into the classroom, and used them to pull toy chariots across the floor, causing much laughter. One day a white mouse fell into an inkwell and was brought out dyed black!

Charles had a bright mind, and made good use of his years at the academy. When he was fifteen, he left school and went to work as a clerk in a lawyer's office. Meanwhile, Mr. Dickens was getting along fairly well as a shorthand reporter. His son decided it would be a good idea for him to learn shorthand, too; so he bought a book on the subject, studying it in his spare time.

At last a newspaper called *The True Sun* gave the younger Dickens work as a shorthand reporter. His duty was to take down speeches made in Great Britain's Parliament. His salary was $28 a week, as measured in our money. This was in 1831.

There is an old saying, "Whatever is worth doing at all is worth doing well." Whether or not Charles Dickens knew that saying, he followed the idea of it when he obtained work as a newspaper reporter. He was careful and accurate in taking down the words of speakers in Parliament, and soon his newspaper reports came to be trusted by those who read them.

Dickens might have gone on successfully in the work of shorthand reporting, but there was something in his nature which made him want to try another kind of writing. One day he went to a building which contained the offices of a monthly magazine. He carried with him a short story. Not daring to take it personally to the editor, he dropped it in the box outside. By and by, an issue of the magazine appeared, and Dickens bought a copy. On opening it, he found his story in print! He was so happy, as he said later, that his eyes were "dimmed with joy."

At that time Dickens was twenty-one years old. Later he was given the regular work of writing short stories or "sketches" for the London *Morning Chronicle.* The stories were signed by "Boz" and came to be known as "Sketches by Boz." They were very popular in London, and in 1836 they were collected and published in two volumes. This first work, "Sketches by Boz," appeared when Dickens was twenty-four years old.

Dickens now set to work with an artist named Seymour to prepare the "Pickwick Papers," one drawing the pictures, the other doing the writing. The death of Seymour shortly afterward forced Dickens to choose a new artist, who signed himself "Phiz." The "Pickwick Papers," issued in monthly form, related the adventures of a peculiar and lovable gentleman named Pickwick and of the friends who gathered about him. Only four hundred copies of the first "Pickwick Papers" were sold. For the fifteenth number, however, there were 40,000 advance orders! The success of the "Pickwick Papers" led Dickens to prepare other little monthly booklets to be sold in the stores. He now used his own name as the author, instead of signing himself "Boz."

The "Adventures of Oliver Twist" were published in ten monthly numbers, and also in book form. They made a novel of a sort, and copies were widely sold. To this day "Oliver Twist" is popular. Other books of Dickens include "A Tale of Two Cities," "Nicholas Nickleby" and "David Copperfield," which contains many scenes and incidents drawn from Dickens' own boyhood.

In some of his books Dickens did more than tell a story. He wrote with the hope of making people learn about wrongs which should be set right. In "Little Dorrit" he worked against the idea of putting anyone in prison for debt.

Among other famous books from his pen is "The Old Curiosity Shop." Many thousands of copies have been sold, and it ranks high among his works. What today seems like an odd title was used when this novel was first published. The story appeared, a chapter or two at a time, as "Master Humphrey's Clock." The parts were supposed to be printed weekly, but they were not in all cases issued promptly. In planning the story, Dickens had what he called a "notion" about an old man named Humphrey, who owned "an old queer-cased clock." Humphrey was to find some old writings in a closet where the clock weights were kept, and these writings were to be given to the reader. Later the name of the tale was changed to "The Old Curiosity Shop."

Dickens left notes which show us how the story grew in his mind. One by one the characters took form, chief among them being Little Nell, the dear child whose sweetness was brought out time and again. Trying to finish chapters from week to week, the author, then twenty-eight years old, was not always sure what the next chapter would contain until he sat down at his desk to write. After telling about the death of Little Nell, he wrote to a friend, "It is such a very painful thing to me that I cannot express my sorrow." This gives us an idea of how real the persons in his books sometimes seemed to him. Usually he wrote about real persons, but changed their names in his books.

In London today there is a place called "Old Curiosity Shop," where souvenirs of Dickens and his book characters are sold. Some persons fancy this to be the original shop described in his book.

Another great work of Dickens' is "A Tale of Two Cities." It is based in part on history, and the events are supposed to have taken place during the French Revolution. The hero is a man named Sydney Carton. He is described in a way which shows him to be weak, and many persons might have thought him worthless. Indeed one could hardly think anything else until near the end of the book. Carton's great deed was to give his life to save another man. He did this for the sake of a woman whom he loved but who did not love him.

As a young man, in his early twenties, Dickens was much in love with a girl named Maria Beadwell. She was a banker's daughter, and seemed to hold a station far above him since he had not yet become famous in his great career as a writer. Maria's parents broke up the romance by sending her to Paris. This was a blow to the young writer who had been struggling for success largely because he wanted to win Maria's hand in marriage. From that time onward, he had to find other reasons to work for success.

Some years later, in 1848, Dickens wrote the notable book, "David Copperfield." In it we meet a character, known as Dora, who stood in the author's mind as Maria. She was David Copperfield's young wife, who died after a short period of marriage. Taking the place of Dora in David's life was another character. She was noble and helpful, and married David after he lost Dora.

The book was presented to the public as a novel, but to some extent it is the story of Dickens' own boyhood, youth and young manhood. There are parts which do not agree with his life history, but many other parts are pages from his early career. One famous character, Mr. Micawber, was pictured in a way to make him something like John Dickens, the father of the author. John Dickens was really an easy-going man, often in debt, but he did more to make his life successful than the Micawber in the book.

Dickens seldom talked to anyone about the sadness in his boyhood, but he told a few persons about the year he spent in the blacking factory while his father was in prison. He said that "David Copperfield" contained so much of his own life that he felt pain, at times, in reading it.

When he was thirty years old, Dickens visited the United States, and at the age of fifty-five repeated the visit. Later he wrote a book about his American travels.

The maiden name of Dickens' wife was Catherine Hogarth. She was the daughter of a newspaper editor. Mary, one of the editor's other daughters, died "in the sweet bloom of youth." It was Mary whom Dickens had in mind when he wrote about Little Nell in "Old Curiosity Shop."

Perhaps no other Christmas story has been more widely read than Dickens' "Christmas Carol." It is the tale of a hard-hearted, sharp-tongued old miser named Scrooge who turned into a kindly human being.

Scrooge was a money lender, the master of a counting house. Year after year he had made money, largely through loans to poor persons whose goods he could take if they did not pay him back with interest.

He had grown rich, but he did not give his money to those who needed it, and he used little on himself.

On Christmas Eve a few persons wished him "Merry Christmas!" but he said that Christmas was all "humbug." Returning to his gloomy rooms that night, he was just placing the key in the door to enter when it seemed that he caught sight of the face of Jacob Marley. Marley had been his partner in business, but had died seven years before.

The face vanished, and Scrooge went upstairs where he sat down before a sickly fire. Before long he heard the sound of clanking chains. The "ghost" of Marley came before him, and told him he ought to change his way of life. That night, during a dream, a spirit took Scrooge to the dwelling of Bob Cratchit, an underpaid clerk who worked for him. Mr. Cratchit and his family were poor, but all were friendly and loving. Even a little lame son, Tiny Tim, was as cheerful as could be. Scrooge had other adventures with spirits that night. He was even allowed to see the future, to look upon his own death, and to learn that none would mourn his passing. The dream was indeed a nightmare.

At last Scrooge awoke to a new Christmas Day, and was happy to be alive. Yet he kept the memory of the night, and it seemed to change him into a new man. Quickly he rushed to the home of Bob Cratchit, and told him he would give him back-payments for his work, and more besides.

In years which followed, Scrooge proved fair in his dealings, and was kindly toward people in general, especially to the little lame boy, Tiny Tim.

Dickens died in 1870 at the age of fifty-eight, but his books have lived after him. In his writings, the author left with his readers the spirit of kindness which should live on and on.

MARY MAPES DODGE

MARY MAPES DODGE

A Magazine for Boys and Girls

BORN 1831—DIED 1905

IN THE 1840's there lived in New York City an interesting family with six members—father, mother and four daughters. The girls had never been to school, but they studied a great deal at home. The father of the family, Professor James Jay Mapes, gave them lessons to do, and helped them to learn many things besides their writing, reading and arithmetic. He saw to it that they studied Latin, Greek, German and French, also drawing and painting.

In their spare time the Mapes girls read books, such as "Gulliver's Travels" and "Robinson Crusoe." The one who showed the greatest love for books was Mary, and her father found out that most of all she enjoyed history. One day he came home and told her that he had bought a new set of history books.

"About what country?" she asked.

"About Holland," the professor told her. "The title is 'The Rise of the Dutch Republic,' and the author's name is John Motley."

Soon Mary was deep in the history of Holland. The more she read, the more she liked it. She could hardly put down the books once she had started reading. To follow the struggles of the Dutch people was as much fun to her as to read an adventure story, and she would rather spend her time on something true than on a tale of fancy.

How she admired the Dutch people! What a great thing it seemed to her that they had built dams to keep back the sea! It was really true that many of them lived in houses below the level of the sea!

She learned how Holland had fought against foreign invaders, and it seemed to her that the people were very brave. Yet their work on the dams to keep out the sea caught her interest chiefly. Sometimes the dams had broken, and many had died in the floods. Instead of losing heart after such sad events, the Dutch had set to work to build new and stronger dams.

As the years passed, Mary kept thinking of Holland and reading other books about the country and the people. Perhaps she would have coaxed her father to let her make a trip there, if a more important question had not come up. A New York lawyer, William Dodge, asked her to marry him, and she accepted.

Then followed years of happiness. Two children were born to the couple, both of them boys. The mother loved them dearly, and often told them stories. She did not know then that one of her stories, about Holland and a brave Dutch boy, would turn into a famous book. While the young mother added to this story night after night, her two small sons listened with special interest.

While the boys were still small, the household was saddened by the father's death. This led the family to change its residence from New York City to northern New Jersey. There, in the country home belonging to her parents, the mother lived with her two sons and spent much leisure time with them.

While the boys were at school, Mrs. Dodge would go to a near-by farmhouse, which had been deserted. She had fixed it up as a place for writing. It was decorated with leaves and Florida moss, and was warmed with a stove of the kind Benjamin Franklin had invented. Here she wrote down new chapters in the story about Holland which she was telling the boys.

In the late afternoon or early evening she would relate a new part of the adventures of Hans Brinker, the hero of her story. The boys seemed never to be able to get enough of it.

"If my sons like the story so well," thought Mrs. Dodge, "perhaps other children would like it, too."

So it came about that "Hans Brinker, or the Silver Skates" was printed in 1865. First it appeared as a serial story in a magazine, later as a book. The reading public was delighted with "Hans Brinker" and the author rose to fame, under the name of Mary Mapes Dodge. In later years she wrote other books, but none of them became so popular as the one about the little Dutch boy.

It may seem strange that a woman who had never been in Holland could write a popular book about that country. Mrs. Dodge, however, had studied a great deal about Dutch customs and history. After the book was published, she was able to cross the Atlantic and visit Holland. One of her sons, traveling with her, went into a book shop to buy a book that would give him a clear idea of the life of the people. "If you want a book which gives a fine picture of Dutch life, you should read 'Hans Brinker, or the Silver Skates,' " the owner of the shop said to him.

"My mother," replied the son proudly, "is the author of that book!"

For a while Mrs. Dodge had a desire to write novels for adult readers, but fortunately for boys and girls she decided to give her time to writing for them. The editor of one of the best-known magazines of the day had an idea for a new publication. He felt there was a need for a magazine especially written for children. Knowing Mrs. Dodge, and admiring her work, he asked her to be the editor. The magazine was called *St. Nicholas,* and for thirty years, beginning in 1873, Mary Mapes Dodge was its editor. She filled each issue with the most interesting stories, pictures, poems and puzzles she could obtain. Nothing was too good for her young readers, and they greeted the magazine with great joy.

Rudyard Kipling asked Mrs. Dodge whether she was going to invite him to prepare a story for *St. Nicholas.* "Do you think you can do it?" asked Mrs. Dodge, and the British author answered by writing two animal stories now to be found in "The Jungle Book." Several other stories, which later became popular in book form, first appeared in *St. Nicholas*. "Sara Crewe" was one of these.

Mrs. Dodge was a friend of Longfellow, Whittier, Mark Twain and other famous authors. They were glad to give their best work when Mrs. Dodge asked for a story or a poem.

Mary Mapes Dodge lived in New York City during most of the years she edited the magazine. She spent her vacations in a quaint, rambling cottage in the mountains not far from New York. There she was hostess to groups of writers and artists who delighted in her company.

It was at this cottage in the Catskills that Mrs. Dodge died. She was seventy-four years of age, and for many years had been known and loved by children of the United States and foreign countries. Her magazine had been, and for many years afterward continued to be, the "children's playground" which she had wanted it to become.

LEWIS CARROLL

LEWIS CARROLL

Nonsense About Alice

BORN 1832—DIED 1898

THE FAMOUS RIVER known as the Thames flows through London. If you follow it downstream, you can enter the North Sea. If, on the other hand, you go upstream on the Thames, you can reach the small city known as Oxford. Although small, this city has a special claim to fame. It is the home of a great university. Oxford University is very old; it was founded in the Middle Ages.

In 1862 there was a teacher at Oxford named Charles L. Dodgson. He was thirty years of age and gave lectures on mathematics to the students. He had already written three books on geometry and algebra. The general public thought these books "too dry" or "too deep," but professors of mathematics found them worth while.

On the day our story opens, Dodgson walked away from the college grounds. He planned to do something very different from giving long talks about deep subjects. He was to take a boat ride with three little sisters—Lorina, Alice and Edith. They were members of the Liddell family, and had known "Dr. Dodgson" for many months. They liked him because he made up interesting stories. The stories were odd, but something about them made the children want to hear more.

It was the afternoon of the fourth of July in 1862. The fourth of July is not a holiday in England, but the boat ride proved a joyful one. Dr. Dodgson was fond of all his companions, but eleven-year-old Alice was his favorite.

Hardly had they started to row downstream, when Lorina asked Dr. Dodgson to tell them a story. "Yes," added Alice, "and I hope there will be nonsense in it!"

"Very well," he replied. "The story today will be about Alice. We shall imagine she goes down into the ground and meets with adventures."

The children wondered how a little girl could go underground, but the story-teller simply said that Alice found herself falling down into the earth through a rabbit hole. Adventures quickly came to her, one after another. All through the boat ride, Dodgson kept on with the story. He did not finish it that day, but agreed to go on with it later. The children were anxious for the rest of Alice's thrilling adventures.

As the days of that summer went by, Dodgson made up new chapters, and at length brought the tale to a close. He was glad the children were so much interested, and said to Alice, "I am going to write it down so you can read it whenever you want to do so."

Then back to the Oxford grounds he went, and gave another "deep" lecture about mathematics. Such lectures were to go on, but Dodgson found free time to put the story of Alice on paper. Within a few months he gave the real Alice the hand-made book. Besides several thousand words, it contained a number of pictures which Dodgson himself had made. Alice was proud of the gift, but she little knew the value it would have some day. She was unable to guess that, in her old age, it would bring her a small fortune.

About two years later, a visitor picked up the story and read it to the end. "This is a great story," he exclaimed. "It ought to be printed as a regular book!"

When Dodgson heard this suggestion, he smiled at the idea, but after a time he agreed to let a publisher see it. The result was a printed book, issued in London. Exactly three years after the boat ride on which the story had been started, the author gave a printed copy to Alice Liddell, who was now fourteen years of age.

"You can place this alongside the copy I made by hand for you," he said to Alice.

So it came about that "Alice's Adventures in Wonderland" was published. The author had decided to use a pen name, and called himself "Lewis Carroll." The initials of his real name were C. L. D., and you will notice that he used the first two when he chose his pen name.

Dodgson, at the time, was thirty-three years of age, and had hopes of growing famous in the field of mathematics. No doubt that was the reason he chose a pen name to be put on his "nonsense book." He did not want his real name to be mixed with anything of that kind. As it turned out, he wrote many books about mathematics, but his fame today rests chiefly on his "Lewis Carroll" books. As the years passed, thousands of copies of "Alice's Adventures in Wonderland" were sold. The volume traveled across the Atlantic, and editions were printed for the young readers of Canada and the United States.

It is now time to go back into the life of Charles L. Dodgson, the man who grew famous as "Lewis Carroll." He was born in an English village in 1832, and during his boyhood was greatly interested in animals. More than once he gave a "circus," and worms and snails were among the performers.

When he was fourteen years old, Charles was sent to Rugby. This school was noted for its sports, but the new student cared little about football and cricket. He was most interested in his studies, and soon was at the head of his class.

After leaving Rugby, he went to Oxford, and there proved to be one of the best students. His excellent record led to his being named a lecturer at Oxford. As "Dr. Dodgson," he became widely known for his work in algebra and geometry.

Dr. Dodgson was a bachelor. Having no family of his own, he took special interest in the children of other families. That explains the large amount of time he spent with the little daughters of the Liddell family, of whom we have spoken. "Alice's Adventures in Wonderland" is a fairy story of a sort, but there are no fairies in it. Instead there are animals which can talk, also a man-shaped being called the Mad Hatter, whom Alice met while under the ground.

There is a great deal of magic in the book. Alice found a bottle marked "Drink Me," and when she drank it she became small, with a height of only ten inches. Later she met more magic and reached a height of nine feet! Then she shrank to a point where she was only three inches tall!

Present-day boys and girls do not read "Alice's Adventures in Wonderland" to such an extent as did children of the past. The story is somewhat confusing and is less enjoyable to most children than many of the books now written for them. Yet in its time it was extremely popular, and was sold widely in the early years of the present century. Even today almost everyone knows something about the strange characters.

A second book about Alice was published a few years later. Its full title was "Through the Looking Glass and What Alice Found There." As in the first book, "Lewis Carroll" was named as the author. That name became known to millions of persons, whereas only a few thousand knew anything about Dr. C. L. Dodgson.

LOUISA MAY ALCOTT

LOUISA MAY ALCOTT

A Girlhood in Concord

BORN 1832—DIED 1888

THERE WAS A family in Boston which had known the meaning of being poor. The father, Amos B. Alcott, was a kindly man and was well versed in books, but he had failed as a "money-maker." He had taught school and had given lectures, but had earned barely enough to feed and house his family. Indeed many times the food supply had been all too small.

The Alcott family was made up of four children, besides the father and mother. All the children were girls, and their names were Anna, Louisa, Elizabeth and Abby.

Excitement ran high in the household one night. Answering a knock at the door, Mrs. Alcott found that her husband had come home from a long trip to the west. He had gone away to give lectures, and it was expected that he would bring home a good sum of money.

The four girls heard the knocking, and tumbled out of bed to follow their mother to the door. Aside from their happiness over seeing their father again, they were anxious to know how much money he had earned. After a hearty welcome, they waited for him to speak of his success. At length little Abby, the youngest, asked, "Did people pay you?"

Opening his pocketbook, the father showed his little daughter a dollar and said, "That's all I've brought back, and I lost my overcoat on the way. But I have met people who may help me on a lecture trip in another year."

That was the news, the sad news. Under his smile, the father must have felt almost broken-hearted. Then the mother spoke:

"It is very good that you have opened the way for another year. Since you're safely home, dear, we don't ask anything else."

That gives an idea of the Alcott family; the mother was a woman with a beautiful nature. She would cheer her husband no matter how the troubles of life might gather.

Louisa, the second oldest daughter, observed the love between her parents. All through childhood, she had seen it and it had warmed her heart. Something of that love was to shine through the books she later wrote.

Though poor in money, the family was rich in friends. Ralph Waldo Emerson, the great writer, was one of the friends. Many times he visited the household. Now and then he sat and talked with little Louisa May Alcott and sometimes she went to his home to see him.

Louisa May Alcott

The suburb of Philadelphia known as Germantown was the birthplace of Louisa May Alcott. She was born on a November day in 1832. Two years later, the family boarded a steamboat and made a voyage from Philadelphia to Boston. Sea-going steamboats were not common in those days.

Tiny Louisa was much interested in the big paddle-wheels. Once during the trip she was lost for some minutes, but soon was found in the engine-room.

In Boston Mr. Alcott opened a school, which, for the first few years, was fairly successful. Then the number of pupils fell off. The teacher had new ideas of how children should be taught, and believed in what we now call "progressive education." That was not what Boston wanted. At the end of five years, the school had only four pupils left, and three of these were daughters of the teacher! The school was given up, and Mr. Alcott earned a small living by giving lectures, and by what other work he could find to do. The family fortunes were low, but the parents tried to keep the children from knowing about their worries. A bright and happy spirit was always present in the home.

Louisa was now almost eight. When the family moved to near-by Concord, she was pleased with the change. There the Alcotts lived in a cottage, with a barn beside it.

What a joy that barn was to them! They played in it day after day, and gave plays, such as "Jack and the Beanstalk" and "Cinderella." When Jack cut down the beanstalk in the play, a "giant" would fall from the hayloft, but, landing on some hay, he would not be hurt.

The years at the Concord cottage made a deep impression on Louisa. Many things which happened there were later described in two of her famous books, "Little Women" and "Little Men." The cottage itself was to be called "Meg's first home" in the well-loved story.

Next the Alcotts moved to a farm not far distant, and lived in a large rambling house with other families. The plan was for everyone to live "the simple life," with just enough wholesome food to get along. The farm was called "Fruitlands." Louisa liked some things about it, but felt that there were too many people in the house. She longed for a room of her own, where she could make up poems and write notes in her diary.

When she was thirteen years old, her dream of having a room of her own came true. Her mother had been left some money by a relative, and this was used to buy their own home in Concord, Massachusetts. For two years the Alcotts lived there, and these years were perhaps the happiest of Louisa's life. She played with her sisters and with the children of Nathaniel Hawthorne and Ralph Waldo Emerson. By this time, however, Louisa knew quite well about the hard times her parents were having to pay for food, clothing, furniture and other things. Loving her father and mother dearly, her greatest wish was to earn money so they could live in comfort.

Except for two years at the school where her father had taught,

Louisa had not attended a regular school, but she had been given lessons at home. Each day she had new lessons, and she learned the value of good books. By the end of her "teens" she was a well-educated young woman.

When the family moved back to Boston, she became a school teacher. There were twenty pupils in her class. For several years she taught, and gave most of her earnings to her parents.

Yet teaching was not to be the main work of her life. At the age of twenty, she sent a story to a newspaper, and it was printed. In payment, she received five dollars.

That happy little event marked the start of a career of writing. The career did not blossom all at once; it grew slowly. From time to time a magazine accepted her stories and paid her for them. She was only twenty-two when her first book, "Flower Fables," was published.

After the Civil War broke out, Louisa made a journey to Washington, D.C., and there served as a nurse in a hospital. This gave her material for another book, "Hospital Sketches," and it was followed by a novel called "Moods."

Following the war, she wrote "Little Women," the most famous book of her life. Dealing with her girlhood in Concord, the volume lives today as one of the best loved books for children. In "Little Women" you will find Louisa's sisters, Anna as "Meg," Elizabeth as "Beth," and Abby as "Amy." You also will find Louisa herself, as "Jo."

The money which flowed in from the successful books was welcome to Louisa May Alcott, chiefly because she could use it to pay all family debts, and to supply funds for her parents' comfort. During much of her later life, she lived with them in Concord, in the home called "Orchard House."

MARK TWAIN

MARK TWAIN

A Boy on the Mississippi

BORN 1835—DIED 1910

WHEN SOMEONE SPEAKS of "Florida," we are almost sure to think of one of the large American states, but there are six villages in the United States with that name. One of these is Florida, Missouri, which contained 208 persons at the time of the census of 1940. It never was and probably never will be a large center of population, but it has one great reason for pride—it is the birthplace of Samuel Clemens, later known as "Mark Twain." This fact makes the little village one to be remembered.

The father of the Clemens family was a lawyer, whose work brought him only a small income. The mother was a kindly woman who had a special fondness for animals—at one time she had nineteen cats in her home! Little Sam spent the first four years of his life in the village where he was born. Then the family moved to Hannibal, another village fifty miles away. There were five other Clemens children, two of them girls.

In later years of his life, Samuel Clemens did not remember much about the village where he was born, but he remembered a great deal about Hannibal. Much of what happened there was to go into the books he was destined to write. Sam became the leader of a group of boys who spent much time swimming in the Mississippi, which flowed past Hannibal. Sometimes they built rafts and floated for miles down the river. Among the boys was one named Tom Blankenship. The time was to come when Tom's adventures would be told in a book called "The Adventures of Huckleberry Finn." Some of the things in that volume are not actually true, but many of them are based on experiences which the boys really had.

That is true, also, of the famous book, "The Adventures of Tom Sawyer." There was no boy in the group named Tom Sawyer, but there was one who may be called the "original" of Tom Sawyer. That boy was no other than Sam Clemens, himself. Another character in "Tom Sawyer," drawn from a real person, was Sid. In actual life Sid was the author's brother, Henry Clemens. In writing about this character in his autobiography, Mark Twain said: "It was his duty to report me, when I needed reporting and neglected to do it myself, and he was very faithful in discharging that duty . . . but Henry was a much finer and better boy than ever Sid was."

The boys made journeys to some of the islands which dot the Mississippi. One island in that part of the river is now called "Tom

Sawyer's Island." Another favorite place to visit was a cave near Hannibal. In it were long, dark, winding passages, and lofty chambers with stalactites hanging from the ceiling. It was easy to get lost in the cave because of its many turns. This cave plays an important part in the book about "Tom Sawyer." Although the character called "Indian Joe" in that volume did not really die in the cave, at one time he was lost while wandering around inside. Today the cavern is known as the "Tom Sawyer Cave."

When he was eleven years old, Sam Clemens suffered a heavy blow in the death of his father. This event caused the boy much sorrow. He kept thinking of the times when he had not obeyed his father. He was sorry for some of the things he had done which had brought trouble to the man who was now dead. Mrs. Clemens saw how the boy was losing himself in grief, long after the funeral, and said to him one day: "You can do nothing to change the past. The right thing now is to promise to be a better boy in the future."

Sam promised, and he kept his promise. No longer did he spend most of his free time getting into mischief with the gang of boys. Leaving school because his mother found it hard to support the family, he obtained work in a print shop when he was only twelve. He worked as printer's apprentice on a newspaper known as the *Hannibal Courier,* receiving payment in food and clothes, but no money. This was the usual arrangement for an apprentice at that time. The clothes were old garments which had belonged to the editor. Sam was only about half as tall as the editor and later wrote that the shirts gave him "the sense of living in a circus tent" and added, "I had to turn up my pants to my ears to make them short enough."

Two years later Sam helped one of his older brothers publish a weekly newspaper at Hannibal. One day, as he was on his way home from work, he saw in the street a leaf from a book. It had been part of a volume about Joan of Arc. The youth read the words on the page, and they interested him greatly. He had never before heard about the Maid of Orleans, and now he decided to learn as much about her as he could. Later in life he wrote a long book about this heroine.

That little event has been used to explain another change in the life of Samuel Clemens. He found other books about Joan of Arc and read them carefully. He also started reading histories. In that way he did much to make up for the education he had missed by leaving school.

While he was in his teens, he set out on a journey which took him to New York, Philadelphia and Washington. He earned his living in those cities by working in print shops.

Returning to the Middle West, the youth studied to become a pilot on boats passing along the Mississippi. The pilot was responsible for keeping the old side-wheelers off the many sand bars, and out of the shallows. Telling about his efforts to perform this hard job, he wrote: "If I had known what I was about to require of my faculties, I should not have had the courage to begin. I supposed that all a pilot had to do was to keep his boat in the river, and I did not consider that that could be much of a trick since it was so wide." As a matter of fact he had to learn every bend in over twelve hundred miles of river! It was hard to keep the boats from running aground. To prevent that, tests of the depth of the river were made at frequent intervals. When the cry, "Mark twain!" rang out, the pilot knew that the testing rope showed two marks of depth, or twelve feet. The memory of that call led Sam to adopt the pen name "Mark Twain" which was to become known to millions of people. To this day, he is spoken of as Mark Twain more often than as Samuel Clemens.

Sam's experience on the river gave him the material for one of his best books, "Life on the Mississippi." It presents a colorful picture of American life along the great river about the middle of the past century. Pioneers and outlaws, young and old, white and black, fill the pages of the book with action.

At the age of twenty-six he made a journey to the Rocky Mountain region, and looked for silver in Nevada. In Virginia City, Nevada, he edited a newspaper, and signed some of his writings "Mark Twain."

Mark Twain's success as an author began when he was thirty-five with the appearance of a book called "The Innocents Abroad." Its pages are packed with humor about his adventures during a trip he made through Europe. Although he later served as one of the editors of the *Buffalo Express,* it was his books, not his editorial work, which made him famous.

"The Prince and the Pauper," a story of two boys who change places at birth, has proved popular with young readers. Another volume, "A Connecticut Yankee in King Arthur's Court," tells about a man who was struck on the head by an iron bar and woke up far back in time—in the days of King Arthur. The Yankee had a hard time understanding the life of that far-away period. Mark Twain showed in his story that the glamor of the days of chivalry did not prevent many persons from suffering misery and injustice.

The list of Mark Twain's works is a long one, but certainly among the best of them are those which tell of the region in which he was born. "Tom Sawyer," "Huckleberry Finn," and "Life on the Mississippi" make entertaining reading, and also add to our knowledge of life along the Mississippi River a century ago.

Mark Twain died in 1910, at the age of seventy-four. He ranks as one of the great authors and humorists of American history.

JOEL CHANDLER HARRIS

JOEL CHANDLER HARRIS

Uncle Remus

BORN 1848—DIED 1908

JOEL CHANDLER HARRIS was born in Georgia during the days of negro slaves, and that fact had a great deal to do with his later life. He learned to know the negroes on plantations near his home, and they told him many of the stories which he placed in books years later.

Joel, himself, was no young master of a plantation. Far from it! His family owned no slaves, and had no farm land, except for a small garden space. With the father absent from the household, Mrs. Harris was forced to be the breadwinner, and she worked hard to earn money to pay the expenses of her son and herself. Yet the boy was able to wander about on near-by plantations, and in that way spent much time talking with negro men, women and children.

One of his older negro friends was called "Uncle Ben." Another was known as "Aunt Betsy," and she was especially popular with Joel and his chums because she baked excellent ginger-cakes, and was always quite ready to offer them to the children who happened to pass the kitchen in which she was employed.

When Joel was sent to school, he showed that he had a quick mind. At home he was fond of listening to stories which his mother read to him, and most of all he liked the book called "The Vicar of Wakefield." That volume impressed him so much that he was led to make up little tales of his own, and sometimes he set them down on paper.

When he was thirteen years of age, the Civil War broke out, and the event changed the course of his life. No longer was his mother able to keep him at school. His future was now in his own hands and from this time he had to earn his own living.

Joel was a small but active lad. His hair was reddish and he was freckle-faced. His light blue eyes always flashed with mischief and good humor and many were the pranks he played. He loved animals and, from the time he was a youngster, he could handle horses as well as a trained man.

It was time for the boy to turn to the serious business of hunting a job. One day at the postoffice he picked up a copy of the first issue of a small country newspaper, called *The Countryman*. In it he noticed an advertisement asking for "a boy to learn the printer's trade." Quickly he wrote a letter to the publisher, stating that he would like the place. *The Countryman* was published on a plantation not far from Eatonton. the village where Joel lived. Having been accepted, he packed up what few clothes he had and moved to the plantation.

Joseph Turner, the publisher and editor, received him kindly, and taught him to set type. In those days there were no linotype machines. Each letter for each word had to be picked from a case and placed in a line with the others. It was a long and difficult task to set up a column of type, yet the boy enjoyed the work. Working from copy written by the editor, he did his part in producing the newspaper, which reached a circulation of two thousand copies. Sometimes Joel did more than his part. He often did some composing in his own mind and set in type now and then a paragraph of news or comment. He supposed that his employer did not notice these paragraphs, but it is probable that Mr. Turner observed each one and smiled to himself over the young printer's efforts to be a writer.

There was an excellent library in the Turner home and Joel was allowed to read the books freely. He read a great deal and thus enlarged his knowledge as the months and years went by. He also spent many hours talking with the negroes who worked on the plantation, and from them he heard legends which had been passed down by African ancestors. As he listened to their folk songs and their stories, he caught their dialect and expressions.

The end of the Civil War, and especially Sherman's "march through Georgia," caused the ruin of the little newspaper. Young Harris left the plantation to go to the city of Macon, where he found employment as a printer on the *Macon Telegraph.*

Now seventeen years of age, Joel felt an even stronger desire to write things which would go into print. He was not satisfied merely to set type for articles and stories composed by others. In his free time, therefore, he wrote articles and mailed them to magazines. One of these was sent to *The Crescent Monthly* in New Orleans, and to his amazement a letter came back offering him a post as private secretary to the editor! Quickly he accepted, and spent the next year in New Orleans, working on the magazine and sending "paragraphs" to New Orleans newspapers.

Although the New Orleans work was interesting, Joel at length fell victim to a strong feeling of "homesickness." This led him to return to Georgia and spend several weeks with his mother at Eatonton. The move was fortunate for his career; it led, before long, to a position on the staff of the *Savannah Morning News* at a salary of forty dollars a week. Up to that time he had hardly dreamed of ever earning so much money.

In Savannah, Harris did good work as a writer, and soon became known for his clever paragraphs and other compositions. In his own mind, however, the most important thing about the city was the fact that a pretty young woman with sparkling brown eyes lived there. Her name was Esther LaRose. Her father owned several steamboats which paddled between Savannah and port cities of Florida. When Harris was twenty-four years of age, he and Miss LaRose were married.

A few years later, Savannah suffered an epidemic of yellow fever, and fearing for the two small children who had been born to them, Joel and his wife decided to move to Atlanta. It was in Georgia's capital city that Harris was to find the chief anchorage of his life. There it was that he joined the staff of the *Atlanta Constitution*, and there it was that he produced the famous "Uncle Remus" stories.

After reading a magazine article about negro folklore, Harris asked himself, "Why should I not write down some of the negro songs, legends and myths which I have heard?" Acting on the idea, he began to write a series for the newspaper on which he was working. He made believe that an old negro named "Uncle Remus" was speaking, and soon thousands of readers were waiting with interest and impatience for more and more of the same kind of stories.

When asked about the original of Uncle Remus, Harris said that he had known an old negro with that name, but he had gathered the stories and songs from "several old darkies," not from just one.

Week after week, month after month, Harris wrote about the adventures of "Brer Rabbit" and "Brer Fox." One of his best-loved stories was entitled "The Tar Baby." In the course of time, people from far countries were sending letters to him, and learned professors in colleges were asking him to explain certain points of negro folklore.

So much interest was shown that Harris began gathering his newspaper writings for publication in book form. The first volume was given the title of "Uncle Remus: His Songs and Sayings." Later came other books, including "Nights with Uncle Remus."

For twenty-four years, Harris remained on the staff of the *Atlanta Constitution*, where his work played a part in building the name of that newspaper. He died at the age of fifty-nine, a man dearly loved by his own children and grandchildren as well as by the countless children who delight in the stories of "Uncle Remus."

ROBERT LOUIS STEVENSON

ROBERT LOUIS STEVENSON

He Dreamed of Being A Writer

BORN 1850—DIED 1894

"MY SON IS a failure."

The father of Robert Louis Stevenson held that opinion when his son was a young man; but later events proved that the opinion was a mistake.

The elder Stevenson was a successful engineer and well-known as a lighthouse builder. He wanted his son to be an engineer, too, but Robert did not greatly enjoy his engineering studies at the University of Edinburgh. His dreams were dreams of becoming a writer.

As a child, Robert was frail and sickly. He could take little part in sports with other boys. Some of the boys were unkind enough to make fun of him. He always loved the outdooors and spent as much time as he could digging out a cave or a house, building a fire and cooking apples in it. He called this "being like Robinson Crusoe."

At home the child was petted and, as the saying goes, "spoiled." A nurse took care of him—a very good nurse. She wrote down the little verses and jingles which he made up during days of illness spent in the garden beside his home. He knew the excitement of watching for the lamplighter at tea time after a long quiet day indoors. Many times he must have had to amuse himself with make-believe battles on his counterpane and long voyages in a boat that was really his bed. In later years Stevenson used some of the verses and jingles which he composed during his childhood in the book, "A Child's Garden of Verses."

The books by Stevenson might never have come from his pen except for one thing—his ill health. He turned toward writing because he could not do what he at first planned to do. Fortunately, he was a gifted story-teller.

Men who make a success of their lives have a certain skill. They know how to turn defeat into victory. When they suffer ill fortune, they in some way work out a new plan, and often find it better than the one which failed.

As a young man, Stevenson studied civil engineering and law. He was admitted to the bar, but ill health and lack of strong interest in the subject made him give up the law. At twenty-five he decided he would be a writer.

At college, Stevenson did not dress like the other students. He wore an old velvet jacket and shabby trousers. Some of the students called him "Velvet Jacket." The story is told of another famous British author, Andrew Lang, who some years later did not wish to be seen in the company of Stevenson when the two met on a fashionable London street. Under a great black cloak that might have covered one of his own pirates Stevenson wore a flaming red tie and a black shirt. A velvet smoking-cap topped off the strange costume.

After leaving college, Stevenson went to France in search of better health. His lungs were weak, and until the end of his life he suffered from tuberculosis. There could hardly have been a worse climate than that of Edinburgh for Stevenson to live in and eventually he had to leave.

Although he suffered from a dread disease, he was brave. To the small strength of his body, he added the mighty power of his spirit and fought the good fight.

Before this time the young Scotsman had shown some skill in writing. He had prepared articles for magazines, but had treated writing as a hobby rather than as a life work.

Meeting people of many kinds, and viewing new scenes, Stevenson came to spend more and more of his time in writing down his thoughts. He tells exactly how he trained himself in the art of writing. Whenever he read a book or a piece of writing that he liked, he tried to imitate it. He says that he was never successful, but the frequent attempts gave him the practice he needed. Since he was, first of all, a born story-teller, it was not long before he became a writer of fame.

At the age of twenty-eight he wrote a book about his travels in a canoe in France and Belgium, calling it "An Inland Voyage." The next year another book, "Travels with a Donkey," was published.

In France he fell in love with an American woman, Mrs. Osborne. After she returned to her home in California, he decided to cross the Atlantic and visit her. The trip was long and hard, but it ended in a very happy marriage. Mrs. Osborne had a young son, Lloyd, who grew to love his stepfather dearly. They were always close and happy companions.

The first book which brought great fame to Stevenson was "Treasure Island." It was accepted in 1881 by a publication called *Young Folks*. People thought it was the best thing of its kind since "Robinson Crusoe." It tells a story of pirates and hidden treasure and has been a delight to many boys. It paints a vivid picture of the sea and creates "flesh-and-blood" desperadoes such as Long John Silver. Grown-ups, too, find it interesting.

Five years after the appearance of this successful book, Stevenson published the novel he considered his best. It is called "Kidnapped" and tells the adventures of a boy named David Balfour. His miserly and wicked uncle caused him to be kidnapped so he could be sent to America in a small sailing ship, there to be sold into service. He was cast away on a desert island, but finally joined Alan Breck Stewart in a plot to restore the Stuart kings to the British throne. There is much excitement before David's uncle is brought to terms, and David is restored to his rightful place.

One night Stevenson had a very strange dream. Upon awakening, he wrote quickly what he remembered. It turned out to be a story about the good and evil sides of a man and is called "The Strange Case of Dr. Jekyll and Mr. Hyde." It was read in many parts of the world and made such a deep impression that a sermon was preached on it in a great church in London.

"The Master of Ballantrae" is another of his famous novels. It is the story of two brothers of a noble family. The scene which people remember best is a duel between the brothers.

In spite of constant illness Stevenson was able to write many short stories as well as articles for magazines. Letters he wrote to his friends and relatives have been published and they show what a brave and kind-hearted person he was.

Much of the time Stevenson wrote while lying in bed. Today in Edinburgh we may see a sculpture of him on his invalid couch in Samoa, where he spent his last years.

In his thirty-ninth year, in 1889, Stevenson went to the island of Samoa, in the Pacific, where he lived until his death five years later. The Samoans liked him very much, and called him "Tusitala," meaning "Teller of Tales." They also spoke of him as the Great White Chief. On the island he wrote "Ebb Tide" and other stories about South Sea life.

If you were to visit the island of Upolu, in the Samoan group, you might find a pathway which the natives cut through the forest many years ago. It is called by a name meaning "Road of the Loving Heart," and was made for Robert Louis Stevenson.

Stevenson bought a piece of land at the foot of a mountain, and there lived in a home of Samoan style. The natives found him always friendly and interested in their well-being. It was in this Paradise among his many native friends that Stevenson died one evening while chatting with his wife. The sorrowful and faithful natives carried him to his grave in a beautiful spot on the top of the Samoan mountain beside which he lived, and on his tomb are carved words which he wrote himself:

Under the wide and starry sky
Dig the grave and let me lie.
Glad did I live and gladly die,
  And I laid me down with a will.
This be the verse you grave for me—
Here he lies where he longed to be;
Home is the sailor, home from sea,
  And the hunter home from the hill.

KATE DOUGLAS WIGGIN

KATE DOUGLAS WIGGIN

Everybody Fell in Love with Rebecca

BORN 1856—DIED 1923

ONE BRIGHT MORNING, youthful Kate Smith boarded a train, in company with her mother. It was the start of a trip from Hollis, Maine, to Portland and Boston. No one at that time had heard of this eleven-year-old girl except her relatives and friends. So far as Kate knew, the world never would hear a great deal about anything she was going to do.

As she rode toward Portland, her mind was not on herself, but on a great man. Charles Dickens, famous English author, was at that time in the United States, and was visiting different cities. That very evening he was going to be in Portland.

When the train reached the Portland station, Kate and her mother stepped off. They were to make a "stop-over" there that night. The little girl had already read most of Dickens' books, and she looked upon him as a hero. She hoped that somehow she might happen to see him on a Portland street.

Such good fortune failed to come, and next day she was on the way to Boston. She did not know that Charles Dickens was aboard the same train until there was a halt at a station. Looking from the window, she saw a man on the platform—a man who looked like a picture of Dickens which she had seen. He had stepped off the train to stroll about for a minute or two, and the child watched him with wide-open eyes.

When "All aboard!" was called, he returned to the train, and Kate noticed that he went into the car next to her own. Her mother allowed her to go into that car, and there she found an empty seat, near the one occupied by the author. He was talking with another man, who sat beside him. Before long, the other man left the seat, and Kate lost no time in taking the place left vacant. Within a minute or two, she felt she was in a dream world. She was talking with Charles Dickens!

Delighted as she was, Kate Smith was perhaps no more pleased than Dickens himself. From the lips of the little traveler, he heard of her joy in his books. She told him that she had read "David Copperfield" six times.

So it came about that the small American girl met the famous British author. Dickens later told a newspaper reporter about her, and the story of the meeting was published in a Boston newspaper. It would have been an even more interesting story if the reporter had known that Kate (under the name of Kate Douglas Wiggin) was herself to become a noted writer.

At eighteen, Kate was on her way to California. Most of her life she had lived in Maine, but lately she had been attending a boarding school in Massachusetts. Now she was on her way to the Pacific coast to join her mother and stepfather, who had made the long journey ahead of her.

In those days young women seldom traveled alone, and Kate Douglas Smith was chaperoned on this trip. Her companion was an elderly naval officer who had retired from the navy; he was now on his way to a Nevada ranch. Leaving the train at a Nevada station, he bade Kate farewell.

When Kate reached San Francisco, she found herself with two trunks filled with the officer's clothing! Meanwhile her friend had gone to his ranch with the trunks containing Kate's dresses!

When Kate's stepfather met the train, the first thing he had to do was to start the baggage back to its rightful owner. Then he escorted Kate south to Santa Barbara without her extra dresses.

Unfortunately, her stepfather died a few years later; he had always been kind to his two stepdaughters, Kate and her younger sister.

Now came a great need to earn money, since the family was in debt. Kate obtained work playing the organ at a church, with a salary of fifteen dollars a month. She knew a little about the piano, but until then had been a stranger to the organ. Yet she was able to keep the position.

She knew that such a small income would be too little to pay family expenses, so she began to train for other work. She entered a school which had just been started to prepare young women to teach in kindergartens. That was in the year 1877.

Before this, Kate had found time to try her hand at writing. She prepared a story, with the title of "Half a Dozen Housekeepers," and mailed it to *St. Nicholas* magazine. Back came a letter saying it would be published, and a check was enclosed! At first, when she looked at the check, she thought the amount was $1.50—very little even for a short story. Looking again, she found that the amount really was $150, and she could hardly believe her eyes.

A year after starting to train to be a kindergarten teacher, she received an offer to open a kindergarten in San Francisco. In company with Nora, her younger sister, she moved to the Golden Gate city. In San Francisco, she made a success of her work as a teacher. She loved the small children in her class, and worked hard to give them enjoyment and good training. With the help of her sister, she prepared programs of songs and games.

At the age of twenty-five Kate married Samuel B. Wiggin, a lawyer. That is how her name came to be changed to Wiggin. Books from her pen were to come forth under the name of "Kate Douglas Wiggin." One book was published two years later, "The Story of Patsy." Three thousand copies were sold, and the sale brought money to enlarge the kindergarten.

For several years, the young woman found it hard to decide

whether to give her life to writing or teaching, but at length she chose writing. At the age of thirty, she wrote a book called "The Birds' Christmas Carol." It is the story of a little lame girl named Carol Bird, the child of a rich family, and of the Ruggles family, large but poor. Many baby girls were named for Carol Bird.

The volume was written during a Christmas vacation period, and this time the purpose was to raise funds to start a new kindergarten. People read the book with interest, and many thousands of copies were sold. Kate Douglas Wiggin came to be known far and wide over the United States.

Following eight years of married life, her husband died. After this sad event there came years in which her restless spirit made her feel the need of travel. She crossed the Atlantic and visited the British Isles. Later she made other voyages to Europe after having married again.

During her travels, and in the periods between, she kept on writing. She had a rich store of ambition, but her health was not always equal to her spirit. Time and again she spent months in hospitals and health resorts, but even there she found time for writing. While she was in a southern health resort, she started her most famous book, "Rebecca of Sunnybrook Farm." Published in 1903, it quickly rose to fame and more than a million copies were sold. It soon appeared on the stage, and not long after, it was made into a moving picture. The book has been translated into several languages.

Among children and grown-ups alike, Rebecca is perhaps the most popular of all Kate Douglas Wiggins' creations. People all over the world fell in love with her; in fact, one man out West telegraphed he would come East and propose to her if Rebecca was not already married.

Kate Douglas Wiggin lived until 1923. Her love for children and her kindness toward them built a monument to her life.

JAMES M. BARRIE

JAMES M. BARRIE

He Created Peter Pan

BORN 1860—DIED 1937

WHEN SIR JAMES M. BARRIE died, he had reached the age of seventy-seven, and had won great fame. From his title of "Sir," we might suppose he had been blessed by fortune at birth, but his family was far from being rich. His father was a weaver in a small town in Scotland, and not much money came into the household. What money there was had to be spread out thinly, since James was one of ten children. The honor of knighthood came many years later, as a reward for Barrie's skill in writing. At the time he was born, even his fond mother had no idea that such a title would be won.

There was little fortune, in the sense of money, in that Scottish household, but there was something else of greater value. The father of the family was a kind-hearted man, always ready to do his duty. The mother was a woman about whom books might be written—and indeed they were! When the son grew up, he told of her time and again. One volume was to bear her maiden name, Margaret Ogilvy, and others were to show her as a much-loved character in stories and plays.

All through his boyhood and youth, Mrs. Barrie gave her son time and love, and he richly returned her love. There was a great store of playfulness in the mother, and James entered into the spirit of her play. Neither of them spent too much time worrying about the hard facts of life.

It may seem strange that James, as a member of such a family, was able to obtain a very good education, but he did. He went up through college, and graduated with the degree of Master of Arts. One might think that a good fairy must have waved her magic wand to allow him to have all that, but let us take a glimpse of him at the University of Edinburgh. There he was one of the many "poor students," not poor in his studies but poor in the world's goods. A few years later he wrote about such students, saying that three of them "lodged together in a dreary house at the top of a dreary street." He added that the three students had only one bed, and had to take turns sleeping in it. While one student was asleep, the other two studied their lessons.

The much-loved mother had wanted her son to become a minister of the gospel, but to this plan James would not agree. It was one of the few times in his life when he was unwilling to follow his mother's wishes. "I am going to become an author," he declared. When he told his mother he wanted to go to London to start his career as a writer, she grew fearful of his future.

"Many young men have tried that," she said, "and most of them have failed. You may starve if you go to London without having a regular job there."

The young man tried to make his mother see that London was not to be feared so much. He spent many hours telling her of the interesting places in London, and suggested that he might even become a close friend of Lord Tennyson, the great poet.

Mrs. Barrie could enter into the dreams of youth, but she was glad when her son decided to go to the city of Nottingham, instead of to London. At Nottingham he was offered a position on the staff of a newspaper. For two years he lived there, writing for the newspaper, and mailing articles to London papers. At last one of his articles was accepted by the *London Illustrated News,* and others were taken by a magazine printed in London. Feeling that he was now on solid ground, he moved to London. He was then twenty-four years of age.

London life proved exciting, but his path was far from easy. Without a regular job, he found on many a day that his purse was empty. Articles and stories from his pen were not always published, and there were moments when he wondered whether he had been wise to move to the big city.

As time went on, however, he met better fortune. He made friends with men who worked on magazines and newspapers, and more and more of his work was published. His first novel had the odd name of "Better Dead." It was a small book, but he was very proud of it. For the first week he carried a copy in his coat pocket everywhere he went. Not many copies were sold. The author tells us of watching "a pretty girl" look at it in a book shop. She read a few pages and he was hopeful that she would buy the book, but at length she laid it down with a smile and walked away.

At the age of thirty-one, Barrie met his first success with a novel. It was called "The Little Minister," and thousands of copies were sold. Later he turned it into a play. When he wrote the volume, he probably was thinking of the time his mother had asked him to be a minister of the gospel. He had refused to follow her wish, but in "The Little Minister" he was able to make believe that he had done as his mother had desired. The minister in the novel was a youth only twenty-one years of age, and he preached in a Scottish village. The people in the village watched the young minister with close interest. They were shocked when he fell in love with a gypsy dancing girl and married her. As a result he came near to losing his place, but he proved himself a hero during a flood and was forgiven by his congregation.

Barrie's mother was alive when "The Little Minister" was written. She enjoyed the book, and thought there was no other author who could write as well as her son.

The mother, however, died before her son produced his most famous work, "Peter Pan." It was a play, and was presented on the stage for the first time on December 27, 1904. The author feared it would be a failure, but the London crowd greeted it with pleasure, and it was performed again and again. It was as a writer of plays that Barrie was to gain his greatest fame.

The next year "Peter Pan" appeared at a New York theater, and had a run of eight months. People liked "the boy who wouldn't grow up." Since that time, the play has been seen in thousands of cities and towns. Some years ago it was made into a talking moving picture, and as a book it is one of the best loved of all fairy stories.

Although adults enjoy "Peter Pan," it is classed as a work for children. Barrie was pleased that boys and girls liked it so well. As a surprise for the children of London, he caused a statue of Peter Pan to be made, and one night it was secretly placed in a London park called Kensington Gardens. On the next morning—the morning of May Day—those who visited Kensington Gardens saw the statue for the first time.

After his success with "Peter Pan," Barrie wrote various other plays. One of these was called "Dear Brutus" and another "A Kiss for Cinderella." His plays were published in a single volume in 1929. When he died in 1937, he had spent almost all his grown-up life in London. He had gone there as a young man "to become an author," and his dream had come true.

RUDYARD KIPLING

RUDYARD KIPLING

He Made the Animals Talk

BORN 1865—DIED 1936

A SMALL BOY of English parentage took a walk alone one day in India. He was hardly four years of age, but he knew the way to the school in Bombay where his father taught art. Suddenly a large hen came from the edge of a small valley, and sprang at him. Running as fast as he could, he escaped; and when he reached the school he told his father of the event, sobbing as he spoke.

Many a child has kept an early fear through life, but John Kipling, the father of this child, did a wise thing. He wrote a little verse:

There was a small boy in Bombay
Who once from a hen ran away.
When they said, "You're a baby,"
He replied, "Well I may be:
But I don't like these hens of Bombay."

Before long little Rudyard Kipling was laughing about what had happened. Late in his life he said: "I have thought well of hens ever since."

India was Rudyard's birthplace and he lived there during his first five years. In that period he had native nurses who told him stories about jungle animals, and these stories he did not forget.

Another important thing about his early years is the fact that he learned to speak Hindustani. This is the most widely-used language in India. When he returned to the country years later, he was able to pick it up again.

There was to be a long period in his life in which he saw no more of India. He was to spend most of his childhood in England.

In company with his father and mother, Rudyard traveled toward England aboard a paddle-wheel steamboat. That was in the year 1871. The Suez canal was not in use at the time; so the Kipling family boarded a train to cross a desert at the edge of Egypt, to reach another seaport. Then another vessel took them the rest of the way. In England an old sea captain and his wife were given care of the boy, and he lived at Southsea for the next six years. His parents returned to India, where the father went on with his teaching.

For a time Rudyard was treated fairly well. The sea captain was kind to him and took him on long walks. One day he was shown a sailing vessel which had come back from a trip to the Arctic. The captain's wife was of a different nature; she was ill-tempered, and mistreated the lad from India.

While at Southsea, England, Rudyard Kipling was sent to "day school," and learned reading, writing and arithmetic. From time to time, letters came to him from his parents in India. and they also sent him interesting books.

Before long, unhappily, the sea captain died, and Rudyard's life outside school became miserable. The captain's wife showed her ill-temper more than before, and cuffed the lad around with little or no excuse.

If Rudyard had written to his parents about his bad treatment, he no doubt would have been placed in another household. As it was, he seems to have felt that this was the kind of life he was supposed to have.

He did not even complain to his aunt when he visited her during school vacations. He enjoyed himself to the limit during a month at her home each year, then went back to the Southsea house. Meanwhile, he had learned to love books, and many a spare hour he spent in reading.

At last his mother came from far India to visit him. He was at this time eleven years old. Mrs. Kipling found out about the bad treatment, and quickly took him away from the Southsea house. For months he enjoyed her company, and felt that "heaven on earth" had come to him.

Having to return to her husband in India, Mrs. Kipling was very careful to leave her son in a better household. Three kind-hearted women, who lived together, took care of the boy after she left. Soon

Rudyard was a student at a new school. He was the only boy there who wore glasses. Although he was teased somewhat, he found good friends at this school. His poor eyesight kept him from taking much part in sports, but he wrote poems and essays which brought him some praise from his schoolmates.

The fun, the torments, and the school-boy pranks must have been remembered clearly years later when Kipling wrote "Stalky and Co." This is a story about English school life. Many boys read the book today and discover the wide difference between their own school days and young Rudyard Kipling's.

At sixteen young Kipling went back to India. There he worked on a small newspaper. When only twenty-one, he became assistant editor of the *Allahabad Pioneer* and soon afterward published several of his famous stories, including "Plain Tales from the Hills,' "The Phantom Rickshaw" and "Wee Willie Winkie."

He also wrote poetry, some of it about India. A favorite poem with many people is "Gunga Din." It is a heroic story of a brave Indian water-boy who was shot while carrying water to wounded British soldiers in the thick of battle in India.

By the year 1892 Rudyard Kipling was a successful young author. He had written books which were widely read, and had a large sum of money in a bank. He had been married in London, England, to an American woman and was on his way around the world. The couple had crossed the Atlantic, and had enjoyed pleasant days in various parts of Canada, including Vancouver

Leaving Vancouver, they had steamed over the Pacific to Japan. Life seemed most pleasant to them, until Kipling went to a bank in Yokohama, a branch of the British bank where he had placed his savings. He had visited the branch bank before, and had drawn money, but this time there was a sign on the door. It gave notice of the failure of the bank in England.

Now came the question of what to do.

"Why not make our home in the United States for a while?" suggested Mrs. Kipling. "I know a place where we could live cheaply."

Tickets clear around the world had been purchased, but a refund was obtained. There was enough money to buy passage to the United States, with several hundred dollars left over.

So it happened that Rudyard Kipling settled with his wife in a Vermont village, where two of his wife's grandparents had lived years before. They rented a house for ten dollars and called it Bliss Cottage. In that dwelling their first child, a daughter, was born.

Kipling was now twenty-seven years of age. Settling down to work, he soon began writing stories which grew into his famous "Jungle Books." The two "Jungle Books" contain stories of wild animals in India, where Kipling had spent about half of his life up to that time. In these books the animals talk together as if they were human beings.

After a short stay in America, Kipling returned, with his family, to England, where he lived until his death in 1936. He was known throughout the world as a poet and teller of tales.

JACK LONDON

JACK LONDON

Adventurer on Sea and Land

BORN 1876—DIED 1916

A GOOD BOOK," it has been said, "is the precious life blood of a master spirit." As we study the careers of great authors, we find that often they have labored long and hard before giving the world a book of a masterful kind. Almost always the writer of such a volume has himself met hardship and suffering.

Surely Jack London was no exception to the rule. San Francisco was the birthplace of this boy who as a youth was, for a time, a homeless wanderer. Yet he stored in his mind a wealth of experience and put into books the adventures he lived through. The name of London was that of his step-father, for whom Jack had a deep affection. His step-sisters, some years older than himself, were always devoted to the bright and lively boy. The family, however, was usually poor and often hungry even though the father did his best to earn a living.

As soon as he was able to do so, Jack took on a newspaper route and in that way earned a small sum that could help to pay the household expenses. Although he was born in San Francisco, the Golden Gate city, the family had moved across the bay to Oakland when Jack was small. It was here that he was sent to school.

One day at school, Jack found himself in trouble with his teacher because he had told her that he would not join in singing. It was his belief that she did not give the class the right "pitch" for the songs. As a result he was sent to the principal, whose name was Garlick. Mr. Garlick, a man with an understanding nature, studied Jack's problem, and then arranged to have him excused from the music class. As a substitute, he was to spend the same amount of time in writing compositions. There was talent in the boy's writing, and when graduation from grade school approached, he was asked to be the "class historian." A youthful worry about his poor clothing led him to refuse the honor, and for the same reason he stayed away from the graduation exercises. After leaving school, he earned what part of his living he could. While employed at an Oakland factory, he was paid ten cents an hour.

The lad's chief interest soon was centered on boats and salt water. There was no such wondrous thing as an ocean voyage for him at that time, but he obtained a small skiff and fitted it with a sail. Using the skiff for fishing, he made exciting trips to various parts of San Francisco Bay.

At the age of seventeen, Jack took part in what was to be one of the great adventures of his life. He obtained employment as an able-bodied seaman aboard the "Sophie Sutherland," a sealing vessel which was bound for waters around the western end of Alaska. A happy day it was when he sailed out on the broad Pacific, aboard a schooner with sails full to the wind. Each task which was given him, he performed with a will. Among the sailors on board were rough men, who were ready to quarrel, and more than once he had to defend himself with his fists. Although young, he was strong, and before long the sailors learned to let him alone. Several among them became his good friends.

Reaching the islands where seals were to be found, the men set to work capturing as many as possible. Jack did his full part, cheered by the knowledge that a large haul of seal skins would earn him more money at the end of the voyage. Before returning, the "Sophie Sutherland" sailed to Japan, and for several days lay at anchor off Yokohama, an important and busy city which serves as a seaport for Tokyo, the capital.

Back in Oakland, Jack received his pay and gave nearly all of it to his family. It seemed to him that his parents needed the money more than he did. The next year one of his shipmates asked him to join in a voyage to the same area aboard another schooner, the "Mary Thomas." He said that he would not go, because, if he sailed again, he wanted to head for the South Seas. So the "Mary Thomas" left port without him, and was never seen again, no doubt wrecked during a storm with all hands lost!

In Oakland, Jack found work in a jute mill, and labored hard for small wages, thirteen hours a day. Hearing of a prize contest being conducted by a newspaper, he set about writing an account of an adventure he had had on his Pacific voyage. He hardly slept for three nights while he wrote at top speed. To his joy, he received first prize, the sum of twenty-five dollars, and his story, called "Typhoon Off the Coast of Japan," was printed in the *San Francisco Call.* He was greatly encouraged.

At about the time he was eighteen, young London became what he described as "a tramp." Working only now and then along the way, he made his way to Washington, New York and Boston, and then returned to his native state.

That much tramping was enough for the time being, and he felt that, if he were not careful, his life would prove useless. In this frame of mind, he decided to go back to school, and at the age of nineteen, became a high school freshman. His father lately had met with better fortune, having become a policeman, and was able to provide food and shelter while the youth studied. Finishing high school within two years, Jack went on to the University of California and spent a year in earnest study, taking as many English courses as possible. In other times, he might have kept on with university work until he graduated, but the Klondike gold rush started in 1897, and he joined it. In company with a brother-in-law, he traveled to Alaska, then to the valley of the Yukon River.

Although the trip to the Klondike was filled with adventure, Jack

London failed to "strike it rich." Like most others in the Gold Rush, he came back poorer than when he had left home.

During the next few years, however, he began to win success in the field of writing, thanks in large part to his memories of Alaska. In 1903 he wrote a book, "The Call of the Wild," which became popular all over the United States. It was followed by many other volumes including "The Sea Wolf," "The Iron Heel" and "The Valley of the Moon."

London had written one short dog story and decided to write another. Once he had started, however, he simply could not stop. The short story soon became a long one. His imagination was strong and vivid. For a whole month he neglected everything and everybody. After only thirty days "The Call of the Wild" was finished. It is about a dog who remained loyal to man until the wolves called him back to the wild life. Jack read the story aloud to some friends and, when he finished at one o'clock in the morning, he could tell from their faces that he had written a good story. Almost immediately it was bought by a magazine for $2,000.

At the age of twenty-eight, Jack London was asked to go to the Orient as a correspondent for a San Francisco newspaper. There he covered the Russo-Japanese War, and his dispatches were followed with keen interest. One of his newspaper assignments carried him to London, where he lived among the poorest people as one of them. His life, in general, was filled with action, and much of it found its way into his books. After he was sure of his success in the field of writing, he extended his travels. One of his journeys took him part way around the world, and the record of that exciting trip is to be found in a book called "The Cruise of the Snark." He was only forty years of age at the time of his death in 1916, but into his life he had packed a wider experience than comes to many persons who live a much longer time.

Index

Index

Index

Index

Index